SHOCKED

SHOCKED

BREAKING THE STIGMA OF MENTAL ILLNESS
AND THE SILENCE OF SHOCK THERAPY

LISA A. CONWAY, MSW

To request permission, contact the publisher at:
publisher@innerpeacepress.com

ISBN: 978-1-958150-53-5
Shocked: Breaking the Stigma of Mental Illness and the Silence of Shock Therapy
First publication: February 2025

Cover art by Malaika Batool from Maya Book Services

Published by **Inner Peace Press**
Eau Claire, Wisconsin, USA
www.innerpeacepress.com

Dedication

This book is dedicated to my son James, my "Why." He is why I fought for my life. He is why I began to run. He was my strength, and still is. James, I wanted you to know that your mom is strong and always here for you. If Mammasan can run a marathon and write a book despite what I went through, then you can accomplish anything your heart desires.

Acknowledgments

To My Friends and Family

It certainly took a village to not only achieve my goal but it has also been an emotional rollercoaster for my family. Paul, you are my rock. You never left my side and you had to care for me in such a difficult way, crisis after crisis, never knowing what you would come home to. There is no greater love than what you've shown me. Mom, Dad, and Terry, you have always said through this that you "have my back" and that couldn't be more true. From driving two hours several days a week to get me to my treatments to offering me refuge when my brain and body needed a break. Maybe I am wrong but I feel this long crisis has indeed brought us much closer together. How could I ever ask for more?

To My Editor Ellen

I sincerely believe that God had a big hand in me writing this book, including me finding you for my editor. I wanted someone who could understand and express my words just as if it were me. I think we knew early on that this would become more than just a business transaction, but that this would form itself into a beautiful friendship. Thank you for your support and compassion in every step of this process.

Table of Contents

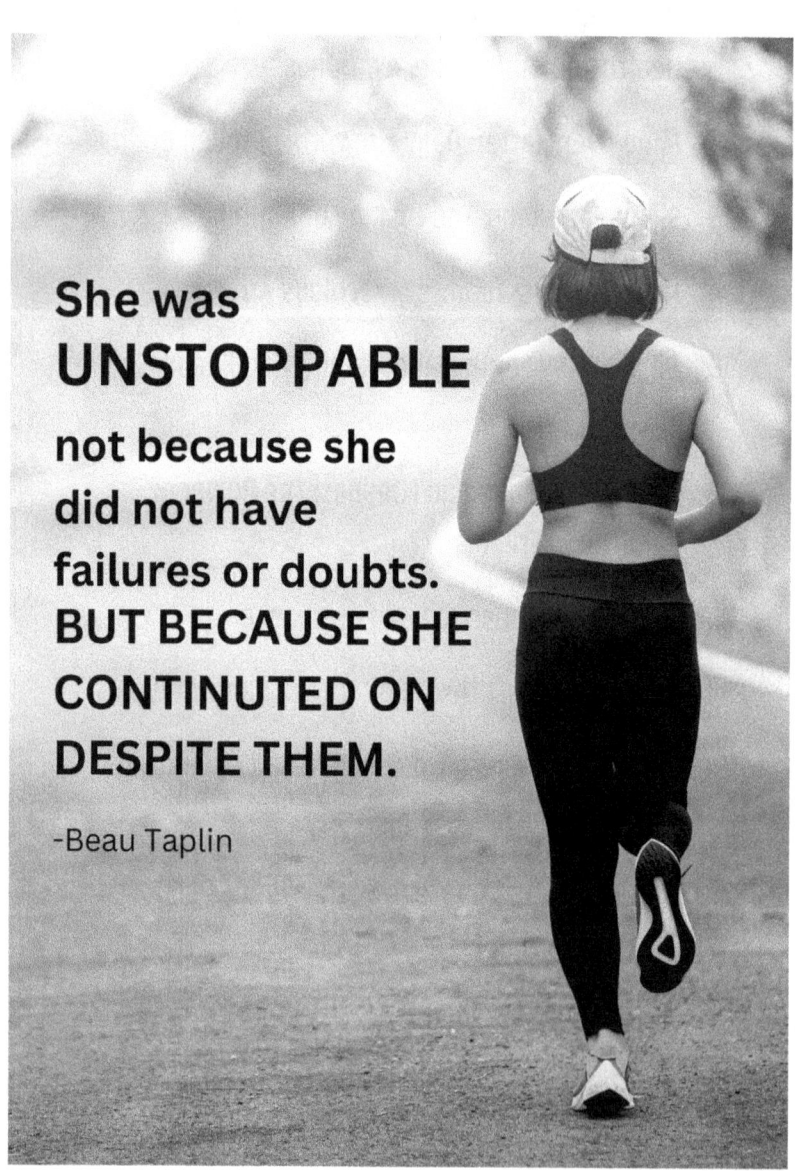

She was
UNSTOPPABLE
not because she
did not have
failures or doubts.
**BUT BECAUSE SHE
CONTINUTED ON
DESPITE THEM.**

-Beau Taplin

Preface

Join me on this extremely painful yet healing journey to uncover the truth about mental illness, depression, and shock therapy. In this vulnerable account, you will read about my experiences with obsessive-compulsive disorder, anorexia, panic attacks, acute anxiety, and bipolar disorder with severe depressive episodes. My encounters with electroconvulsive therapy (ECT) will shock you and provide a chilling look into its effects.

This book is a compilation of personal stories and experiences related to these disorders. In addition to sharing my own journey, it offers insight into the inner workings of someone's mind when struggling with conditions like anorexia, explaining how they perceive themselves as overweight despite weighing only 90 pounds.

You will gain a glimpse into the mind of someone with obsessive-compulsive disorder, witnessing the rapid thoughts and how repetitive behaviors temporarily ease their anxiety. You'll also see into the mind of someone who appears to have a great life yet feels a deep desire to end it. You'll get a clear picture of the profound damage that shock therapy can do to the brain, including its effects on memory, comprehension, and verbal expression, which can dramatically alter one's way of life.

There are no confusing statistics or quotes from famous doctors and psychiatrists here. What you'll find is the true story of someone who, like you, suffers and survives every day, battling to keep the slithering snake called depression from taking over and wreaking havoc. You'll read about the many shock treatments I underwent in my desperate attempt to gain a normal life and how those treatments left me disabled, unable to work, and stripped away 15 years of my memory, gone forever. However, despite it all, there is hope.

You'll also read about how my family rallied together to pull me out of each devastating bout of depression. I'll share the loneliness I felt while staying at home, jobless and without a career, and how I found companionship in my loving service dog, who inspired me to leave behind the isolation of my bed, my lonely home, and my existence in despair. You'll follow my journey as I began walking and eventually running with a local group that became both my support system and source of my closest friends. Finally, you'll read how my amazing service dog and a simple pair of running shoes helped me achieve my lifelong dream of running a marathon, a goal I once thought was impossible due to my complex psychiatric history.

My hope is that this book reaches those fighting psychiatric illnesses and lets them know they are not alone in their struggles. I also hope it reaches families, caregivers, and professionals, offering them a deeper understanding of the thoughts and feelings that accompany these conditions. If this book helps you in any way, please share it with others who might benefit from understanding themselves, or their loved ones, more deeply. Depression is a global issue, one that has only worsened since Covid-19, and maybe this book can help ease the burden for some, improving the lives of those who struggle to make it through each day.

Lisa Conway
Pennsylvania
February 2025

Introduction

I had a happy childhood with two stable and loving parents whose most important goal in life was to raise a healthy family. I also had a fun and energetic sister who was two years older than me. Dad worked in a large bank in New York. He worked with computers and wrote many programs that are still in effect today in the banking world. Mom worked at a preschool as a teacher. She worked with very young children whose parents would take them to school in the morning so they could be well cared for while both parents were at work. The children loved "Miss Flo," and she was thrilled to be part of their day.

Mom and Dad were always around for us. Just like other families, we would play out in the streets on our bikes, play soccer in the front yard, or go to the neighbor's house who had all the cool Barbie dolls. It was a short street with a cul-de-sac at the end, so there wasn't traffic to worry about. My parents would take us to different theme parks, and every summer we played in the pool with our friends; it couldn't have been better. Our childhood was wonderful, so there was no reason to be sad or depressed.

I often find myself wondering: How did my life spiral so far out of control? How did I become depressed, anorexic, and terrified of the world around me at just 15? How have I endured all these years with depression lurking in the background, ready to strike at any moment? And how did I end up spending so much of my adult life in psychiatric hospitals?

I have a very long psychiatric history. It started with obsessive-compulsive disorder around the age of eight. Anorexia followed in high school. Anxiety and depression emerged like unwelcome guests, haunting me for as far back as I can remember. I have been on a myriad of different medications throughout my life, but medications have many side effects. In my 30s, depression reached a stage where I was suicidal and desperate for relief. It was like having an agonizing and life-threatening tumor or cancer and action or surgery was urgently required.

At first, I would be admitted to the hospital because I was so terribly depressed. We had tried everything – various combinations of medications and therapy – but none of it was successful. Our options were depleted. I

urgently needed relief; the consequences would have been dire. My psychiatrist suggested electroconvulsive therapy (ECT), commonly known as shock therapy, because it works rapidly and effectively. With me being in a state of deep desperation, my husband and I agreed.

When we tried to find more information about ECT, everything we read said it was a "safe and effective way to treat medication-resistant depression." It sounded like a good option, in fact, the only option in a situation of hopelessness. I signed the consent form, placing my trust in my psychiatrist, who had helped me through numerous crises in the past. The doctor assured us that it was "safe and effective." He assured us that the only side effects would be a temporary impairment of my short-term memory during the treatments, but that it would return to its normal functioning over time. He also mentioned the possibility of occasional long-term memory issues, also reassuring us that these would gradually fade away with time. Aside from that, we were unaware and not informed of any additional side effects.

Consequently, I had over 100 shock treatments over a period of about 12 years. I think... I'm not sure, as this type of treatment is accompanied by a great deal of memory problems. Many people start off with a series of treatments. Sometimes it starts with three a week for two weeks, then down to two, then down to one. Some people have monthly maintenance treatments. Many times, with those treatments, depression starts to lift, as it did with me. The number of treatments is under the discretion of the psychiatrist; there is no precise "prescription."

You might ask why it is called "Electroconvulsive Therapy." Well, the purpose of the treatments is to make the patient have a grand mal seizure.

"A what?"

"Yes, a grand mal seizure."

"But aren't seizures bad?"

"People with epilepsy are given medicine to prevent them from having seizures because it is known that seizures can cause further damage to the brain."

"Why would someone induce a seizure?"

ECT has been shown to help improve the lives of many people with depression and other disorders, but medical professionals still cannot explain how it works or why it works. In the beginning, after just a few treatments my depression seemed to lift. I was able to return to work and resume daily functioning. The only problem was that my memory had not resumed its old functioning. My psychiatrist kept telling me to "give it time." However, I had a relapse and had to be admitted to the hospital again. We chose to follow the ECT route again because it had been more effective than other treatments. How could I have placed such immense trust in my doctor, permitting him to administer over 100 shock treatments to my brain?

I wasn't even aware that they still did these treatments, and I worked in the medical field! Only years later would I discover how dangerous those treatments were and how they would go on to affect my entire life, making me incapable of continuing my lifelong work as a medical social worker. With this reflection as our compass, let's embark on the path that brought this book to life, guiding you through the story that shaped its pages.

Today

I remind myself to take care of my body, my heart, and my thoughts because I am the only person capable of truly taking care of myself.

Bright Start: Fond Memories of Family and Friends

I have very fond memories of my childhood; it was a joyful time in my life. It was filled with time spent with cousins from both sides of the family. They were, in many ways, our first friends. Every Sunday, we would pile into the car and drive to New York to visit my mom's family. Being part of a large Italian family meant lots of pasta, wine, and animated conversations. I always sat at the kids' table in the kitchen with my cousins. As the youngest of the five cousins, I ended up in a highchair-like contraption. After dinner, we would play cards for hours, both adults and children together. My mom and her mother were particularly skilled at cards, and they were also the ones to watch to ensure no cheating or funny business occurred.

Dad had two sisters. We'd get together with them every month or two. The one family had five kids, so there were always enough people to play ball. They also had a pool like us, so summertime was open season for basically spending the whole day in the pool. It was nice to visit them because the adults would always join in the games and splash around in the pool. Sometimes I think that the adults (especially the uncles) would still play games even if us kids weren't there. It was always like a big party with them.

I remember one time when we drove to visit my dad's side of the family. More members of my dad's side of the family and some fun-loving neighborhood friends joined us on that particular occasion. The one time there were so many people there that instead of one of my aunts slaving over a hot stove all day to feed all the people, my uncle suggested that they should order Chinese food! The only problem was how to cater to everyone's needs and tastes. My uncle didn't want to take the chance of missing anything, so he ordered one dish of everything on the menu! We kids thought that was the most awesome thing ever. One thing you could always count on with both sides of my family was that there was always enough food to fill everyone's bellies.

My parents are still as healthy and strong as ever, and they gave us a childhood that was nothing short of perfect. I see them regularly and cherish our close relationship. They were always friendly with the neighbors and our friends' parents, embodying remarkable thoughtfulness. For instance, if you secretly wished for a particular birthday gift, you could be sure that not only would you receive it, but you'd also get a pleasant surprise.

I remember my 16th birthday vividly. During my sleepover party, my parents suddenly told us to turn up the radio. To my delight, they wished me a happy sweet 16 and dedicated the song *Sixteen Candles* to me. Hearing my name on the radio was a thrill, and my friends thought it was pretty cool, too. My parents complemented each other perfectly, and it was clear that we could never play one off against the other. They were a united front. Whatever Mom said, Dad supported, and vice versa. Our home was always filled with joy, love, and cherished relationships.

I was raised in a wonderful family. Mom and Dad were always there for us to either join in the fun or to put us back in line when we needed to be disciplined. They consistently treated both of us with fairness, ensuring there was never a hint of favoritism toward either me or my sister. We reminisce about one situation when we were young, when she was about ten years old and I was about eight. We had all come home from being out and, after we were home for a little while, my parents called us into the living room to talk to us together. They wanted to know the identity of the culprit responsible for leaving a long strand of toilet paper on the bathroom floor.

Neither of us had any idea what they were talking about, and why bother with such a trivial crime? But being a wife and mother now, I completely understand why they were upset. As a mother spends a lot of time keeping the house tidy, parents expect their children to pick up after themselves and maintain cleanliness without constant reminders. Moreover, wasting toilet paper is no joke. Someone had to fess up; there was no way out of it. So, my sister and I stepped back, huddled, and considered our options. Who would "take one for the team"?

Well, due to "pressure" and "blackmail" from my older sister, I had to take the fall for this minor misdemeanor. At that stage, I still had no idea why this crime was so terrible and that I had to be disciplined for it. All I knew for certain was that I would be disciplined. My sister and my mom stayed in the living room, and my dad took me into another room. I knew I was in big trouble, and my dad was extremely strict. Mom and Dad

always had each other's backs, and they were always on the same page in terms of discipline, even if one of them was in the wrong.

The aim of this story is that I didn't really remember that my dad punished me or that he put the fear of God in me for not cleaning up behind myself, but I remember that my mom and dad stood together and made sure we grew up to be decent human beings. I also appreciate these memories because we were a normal, happy family with unique quirks, and we can laugh about everything now. It is amusing, really, how these particular types of situations strengthened the bond between me and my sister. To this day, we still laugh about the mystery of the toilet paper! My dad was always fun and upbeat. Despite his important job in New York, his absence never left us kids feeling neglected.

I remember that every year he had the whole month of July off. He saved all of his leave days to spend time with us. He was sometimes like a big kid. He loved taking us to theme parks, especially water parks with those exhilarating slides that started at the top of a towering structure and sent you speeding down with just your bathing suit and the big pool of water. We did that every year, and my dad didn't always wait for the kids to go down the slide first. He was more than happy to "try it

out" first before any of the kids went down. It seemed like there was never any lull in his level of energy. He was just as good keeping up with us kids as any of us were.

My mom was born in a small town in Paduli, Italy. My mom was the more serious parent, but she was caring and loving. If you were sick in any way, you definitely wanted her by your side. We all hated it when we were sick and she would bring out the Pepto Bismal tablets. I couldn't stand to chew the pink tablets, let alone their smell. Mom wasn't just around when we were sick. She was like this constant and secure presence, and you always felt safe when she was around. Even if we were playing in the streets, you bet she took good tabs on where we were and who we were with.

Back then, all the parents knew each other, so even if you thought you were getting away with something because you were at a friend's house, you could bet that as soon as you got home she already knew. Your friend's mom had probably called her to report your mischief. Despite being the one who kept us in line because she was always around, Mom could also be a lot of fun. She would teach us how to make paper airplanes, and we'd spend hours taking turns throwing them to see which one flew the farthest.

If it was a rainy day, she immediately had plans for the activities we would do during the day. Sometimes it was a board game, sometimes it was card games, and sometimes it was something that she spontaneously thought of. She was talented in every way possible. She would knit or crochet baby blankets. If we came to her with a broken toy, she had just the thing to fix it. She could fix anything. I still can't figure out how because some of these things were broken pretty badly, but she would come up with some crazy creative way to make it better. She was the one who could do anything. She was a strong Italian woman, and family was her number one priority.

Mom's parents had come over from Italy and started working and earning their keep as soon as they arrived. My grandma worked in a sewing factory, and my grandfather worked as a barber. He had been a barber in Italy. Little by little, they were able to become citizens and then sponsor their children to come over from Italy. After they retired, they stayed with us in the downstairs part of our house. Grandma was spunky but strict, and Grandpa was serious and stern. I learned a lot from them about the importance of giving a project your all and depending on God to see you through your bad days. We were Roman Catholics, so Sunday mass was a must, and we were always dressed properly and prudently.

They said their rosaries daily. It seemed like they did this a hundred times a day. I would go downstairs to get the laundry for mom, and I would see them sitting next to each other, saying their rosaries aloud in Italian. I did not know much about rosaries, just that they should be a part of everyone's day. Interestingly, in the past year, I have turned toward the rosary in desperation for healing and comfort. I always carry my grandma's rosary with me.

My mom was a strong role model for me later in my life. She was the silent one who suffered great sadness when either of her girls was sick or upset. Mom was "sick" herself "once." I remember one Saturday morning when I was 11 years old, returning home from grocery shopping with my mom and my dad and my sister, like usual. As we had a bi-level house, the kitchen was unfortunately and unusually located up the stairs on the second floor. The worst part of grocery shopping has always been to carry all those brown paper bags into the house and then up the stairs to the kitchen.

On this morning, my mom went straight into the house without carrying any bags into the house. This was unusual. My sister and I were left alone to unload and carry all the bags upstairs. Annoyed, I recall saying to my sister, "Why doesn't she have to carry a bag like the rest of us?" The sad answer was that mom wasn't able to carry any bags, let alone make it up the stairs. When we went to check on our parents, Dad was with Mom in their

bedroom, and she was lying in bed. I went back to the kitchen, and my dad came into the kitchen and said, "We have to call 911!"

Suddenly, everything was chaotic. Dad told me to go outside and guide the ambulance to the right place in our house. My sister and I waited in the front yard, feeling anxious. What was happening? Who were these strangers in our home? Was mom really sick? She seemed fine at the store. We had so many questions but no answers. Dad then sent us to the neighbor's house so we wouldn't see what was happening with Mom. We waited there for hours, worried and wondering what was going on. The waiting and confusion ended when we learned that my mom was in the hospital after having a heart attack. At age 11, all I understood was that something very serious had happened. For a long time, I felt guilty about my comment at the car about her not carrying any bags. I couldn't believe how thoughtless I had been.

We didn't get many details, but I recall catching a glimpse of her briefly in what looked like the Intensive Care Unit. She had tubes and machinery hooked up to her, and her arms were completely purple and blue from all the times they had to give her injections and probably insert IVs. It was scary to see my mom in such a state. She underwent double bypass surgery in another state

because our home state hadn't started performing the life-saving procedure yet. The doctors doubted she would live for five more years after the surgery.

Mom survived, and not only did she survive, but she also thrived for the next 40 years. She and Dad recently celebrated their 60th wedding anniversary. She's incredibly resilient considering all she's been through over the years. It was a challenging time, with numerous doctor appointments, cardiac rehab, and strict exercise routines. Even dad took up jogging to shed a few pounds and boost his health. Dad started a regular routine of running every morning, and I thought it was the coolest thing. When I started high school, I asked if I could start jogging with him, admiring him for being so dedicated and diligently doing it every day.

The only drawback was that he would go for a run at 5:00 a.m. I couldn't do this. I loved to sleep; boy, did I love to sleep! I still love sleeping! Dad was determined to have me as a running partner despite my love for sleep. It got to the point where he'd grab my arm and physically pull me out of bed, causing me to hit the floor for a jog. Well, that marked the end of my running days... or so I thought. My father, however, would continue running over the next 40 years.

My dad was a Marine. His grit and determination would help him to go on to run many races. The one that had the most impact on me was the Marine Corps Marathon in Washington, DC. At that race, as I was waiting for my dad, I felt the excitement of all the spectators. They would cheer when their loved ones passed by. I saw the faces of the runners coming across the finish line, exhausted yet simultaneously exhilarated. Many people were running into the arms of their families and crying like babies. They had done it! They had accomplished their goal after months and months of sacrifice and training both physically and mentally. I wanted to be like them and accomplish such a goal. But I had no intention of getting out of bed that early to train so hard. Little did I know how much of an impression that race would make on my life!

My sister was a different story altogether, and I couldn't help but envy her. Always fun and bubbly, she effortlessly made friends and was known for her adventurous spirit. She was the one most likely to push the boundaries and break house rules. Dinner was a family affair in the kitchen, and we always ate as soon as Dad changed out of his work clothes into his Levi's dungarees. Back then, jeans weren't yet in fashion for women. Even now, he still calls them "dungarees." After dinner, it was

my sister's and my responsibility to help wash, dry, and put away the dishes. But somehow, when it was time to tackle our chores, she would mysteriously vanish, often to the bathroom but sometimes elsewhere. So, more often than not, washing all of the dishes was left to me.

My sister Terry was the oldest of all the neighborhood kids and always dictated the games we played. I usually went along with whatever the group decided. Terry had a knack for bending the rules to her advantage. Our allowance came from my father on Wednesday nights after he inspected our rooms. If they met his standards, we received a few dollars. Because of my obsessive-compulsive disorder, my room was always spotless by Tuesday. But every Wednesday after school, Terry would rush to clean her room and beg for my help. Though she managed to get her allowance, she would spend it within days and come to me, knowing I always saved my money. If memory serves me right, she even called me from college, asking me to send her money!

I looked up to my sister, but I couldn't figure out why. What I am trying to say is that she was always pretty bossy. She would push me around, and she even taught me how to throw a punch. Terry had a lot of friends. My mom and dad didn't approve of all of them. That didn't seem to bother her a bit. She did what she wanted

anyway. I really wished that I could be like that, but I was so afraid of getting into trouble with Mom and Dad or disappointing them. I guess that was my big thing: I didn't want to let my parents down.

Consequently, Terry had a blast in high school. She had lots of friends and escapades like going to see an R-rated movie. Truthfully, I think I saw my first R-rated movie with her and her friends. As her senior year graduation approached, she managed to throw a huge pool party in our backyard during school hours. Now, that took guts. My parents were absolutely furious. I wish I could remember how the story ended, but the details escape me.

We lived in a close-knit, friendly town where everyone knew each other. Every day, we walked to school together, waiting at the bottom of our street for the kids from the next street to join us, forming one big group. I have no idea what we did when it rained since there were too many of us to fit into one car. Our journey home was never rushed; we meandered, taking our sweet time and stopping by the local shops for candy and other fun kid stuff. Every Valentine's Day, Terry and I were sure to stop at the florist so we could get a bunch of flowers for my mom. Always carnations. Roses were above our budget. Little League and soccer were the big activities in our town. By late August, we were already signed up for soccer and eagerly waiting to find out which of our friends would be on our teams. Despite not knowing the first thing about the game, Dad volunteered to be a coach. He had grown up playing football in an all-Irish neighborhood, but his enthusiasm and way with kids made him a great coach, even if our stats weren't the best.

I have fond memories of playing soccer, vividly recalling Dad rushing up and down the sideline with his famous clipboard, shouting instructions to the players. I always played defense, enjoying the thrill of guarding the goal and making powerful goal kicks down the field. In my mind, I can still hear Dad's voice yelling, "BOOT IT, LEE!" He was the only one who ever called me that. "Lee" and "Red" were his special names for me, and even now, he still calls me Red, while I call him Dad or Daddy. We've always been very close, and we still are. Reflecting on my childhood, I am filled with fond memories of family, friends, and good times. Yet, despite such a happy beginning, my life would eventually take an unexpected turn into a dark spiral of depression.

Some of the kindest souls I know have lived in a wold that was not so kind to them. Some of the best human beings I know have been through so much at the hands of others, and they still love deeply, they still care. Sometimes, it's the people who have been hurt the most who refuse to be hardened in this world, because they would never want to make another person feel the same way they have felt. If that isn't something to be in awe of, I don't know what is.

- Bianca Sparacino

Dark Whispers from the Pages: Memories Etched in Journals

Despite my happy childhood and fond memories, there were a few unpleasant experiences that would later lead to some of the most challenging moments of my life. One particularly disappointing incident from my youth was the Christmas grab bag event during my third grade year at school. Each classmate was asked to bring in a small, wrapped $5 gift for everyone to exchange gifts. You never knew what you would get, a new pen, a small toy, a coloring book. There were so many possibilities. We all chose gifts. I was thrilled just to tear open the wrapping paper, never mind receiving something awesome.

When I unwrapped my gift, I felt my heart drop into my stomach. It was the ugliest thing I'd ever seen: a misshapen monkey ornament that seemed more suited for the circus than a gift exchange. While everyone else showed off cool toys and accessories, I was stuck with this odd monkey. It really belonged in the garbage.

Disappointed? Never! Despite my memory issues, it's strange that I still recall this monkey story. The fact that I remember this odd monkey thing after all this time surprises me. What's even funnier is that my parents, who've been married for 60 years, still hang that ornament on their tree every Christmas! Now that's a memory I wish I could forget!

It has been a long journey with this mental health challenge. I remember being only eight years old when I started counting. I figured that all the other kids did it in their heads, just like me. When I felt upset, I would count things in my head. I meticulously counted the ceiling tiles, the steps of every staircase in every house I've ever been in, the number of bricks on the patio, and the floor tiles, cataloging every detail present.

It became something that I couldn't turn off in my head, and the more stressed I got, the faster I counted, over and over. T-h-e-n-I- s-t-a-r-t-e-d s-p-e-l-l-i-n-g e-v-e-r-y-t-h-i-n-g i-n m-y h-e-a-d a-s I t-a-l-k-e-d o-r a-s t-h-e o-t-h-e-r p-e-r-s-o-n w-a-s t-a-l-k-i-n-g. I-t w-a-s a c-o-n-s-t-a-n-t r-e-e-l g-o-i-n-g o-n i-n m-y h-e-a-d j-u-s-t l-i- k-e I w-a-s t-y-p-i-n-g i-n m-y h-e-a-d. It was maddening and it creeps up n-o-w a-n-d t-h-e-n w-h-e-n I g-e-t- r-e-a-l-l-y s-t-r-e-s-s-e-d o-r o-v-e-r a-n-x-i-o-u-s. I later learned that it was called obsessive-compulsive disorder. People would be in front of me having a conversation, and I would be spelling their words as they spoke, just in the way that I am typing this book. It's just how my brain works.

When I was upset, I would start counting the desks in the classroom or the books on the shelf. I loved to arrange the books on the shelf from tallest to shortest. I never thought twice about it. It just seemed like the way it ought to be. I loved counting steps in houses. For some reason, an amazing number of houses have 13 steps! I'm not sure why. I grew up in a split-level house, so when you were going up the stairs, there were the first six. Then you got to the landing, and there were seven more. Every time, without a doubt, I was counting those steps. I can't go anywhere without counting the steps.

It's this obsessive mechanism present in my brain that I can't shake. It used to be way worse. I'd get so caught up in counting and spelling that I'd tune out everyone around me. It was like I was typing every word out, complete with commas and spaces, in my head. When I told my psychiatrist, he prescribed the perfect medication to help manage it. Later in life, I found out that I have a cousin with the same condition, but we never see each other, so I never had the opportunity to talk to him about it. I have been on medication for many years that prevents repetitive spelling and counting. It still occurs, but not to the same degree. One positive outcome from my hospitalization for depression was that it addressed at least one issue.

From an early age I've written in a diary, otherwise known as a journal. Grown-ups usually don't keep diaries because it seems a bit immature. Adults keep journals. My very first diary was a Strawberry Shortcake diary. It had a lock and key, and that was crucial because my sister would constantly try to find and read it. I started the habit of writing everything down, not trying to be creative, just to keep track of the important things in my life. To this day, I still keep a journal. Because I have severe memory loss due to the ECT treatments, the journals have been a blessing. Those journals have helped me piece together the things that have happened to me in this life. The journals and conversations with my family have helped me tremendously to recall stories and to write this book.

The majority of entries in my journals stem from periods of depression, loneliness, or sadness. I wrote many of these entries during my stays in psychiatric hospitals for at least 20 years. On a psychiatric ward, there's ample free time to dwell on one's tormenting emotions. Consequently, I found myself instinctively writing down my thoughts and feelings. One of the things about ECT is that your short-term memory is affected. I was always told that it would

return, but it never did. My long-term memory was severely affected as well. So, drafting this book is quite a challenge, trying to put the pieces of my life together once more. I have told my therapist on multiple occasions that my head is like a jigsaw puzzle.

I wake up in the morning, and the pieces are all scattered. It takes most of the day to get the pieces back where they belong. I do this every day, repeatedly. Through journaling, I also recall all the disappointments I faced, such as the monkey gift disappointment. From my perspective, my life was full of disappointments. Others might not see them as significant, but these seemingly trivial matters were actually laying the groundwork for the depression that would affect me throughout my life. Despite my positive upbringing, my mind perceived and interpreted things very differently.

At this very moment, it feels strange trying to write this, considering that just yesterday I entertained thoughts of wishing for a car to hit me. I imagined that it would be a seemingly uncomplicated exit, at least in my mind. To be honest, I have been feeling this way for a while. Life has become quite busy and haphazard, which is when things start to get "a little" challenging. Several years ago, my husband and I began seeing my depression as a type of cancer.

While I didn't undergo chemotherapy or radiation, depression manifested in episodes, coming and going. In remission and out of remission, resembling the cycles experienced by someone battling cancer. Similar to cancer patients, I also had many "treatments." We would notice periods where the depression seemed manageable, entering a sort of remission, yet there lingered an unsettling feeling that it waited in the shadows, poised to reveal its evil presence once again.

I was admitted to the psychiatric hospital a few times. The staff was familiar with me and knew me so well. They were always compassionate and kind. They already knew when I came back that I would say I simply needed a "tune-up." However, despite their kindness, each return to the psych ward added a layer of shame to the myriad emotions accompanying me on this gloomy expedition called "DEPRESSION."

I was a reserved and quiet child. Despite having a close and loving relationship with my sister, I often felt overshadowed by her. I admired and longed to be like her. She was outgoing, surrounded by friends, effortlessly witty, and had a vibrant social life. I was the opposite. I was told more than once that I was "too sensitive." I had bright red hair and freckles, and the other children made fun of me at school. You know the usual mockery:

"Carrot Top," "Freckle-Face," and "Four-Eyes!" It was bad enough that I stood out, but it was made worse by my sister, who I still love and adore, who used to say that I was adopted because there was no one else in our family with red hair. For many years, it tore my heart apart and really hurt my feelings. Now, years later, both of us laugh at how stupid and infantile it was.

High school was gruelingly daunting for me. I felt so intimidated, just by the mere size of the building. It occupied an entire city corner. Throughout junior high, we'd been with the same classmates since kindergarten. Now, it felt like I was tossed into a den of wolves. Every morning my stomach ached at the thought of spending the entire day there. Getting on the bus petrified me even more. Through middle and intermediate school, we always walked to school in a big group.

High school was in the next town. It was a very busy town, so we had to take the bus. We had to get up at a ridiculous hour just to start getting ready to leave the house. I could manage walking to the bus stop, but getting on the bus terrified me. Every day I would wonder whether I would have to sit in the back with the "bad kids," the ones who always got in trouble and smoked, or would I have to sit in the front like a nerd. I never knew what to expect or who else would be on my bus. Luckily, there was a "normal" girl, like me, sitting by the window in the fourth or fifth row. That was a perfect spot for me.

My first experience of the school was completely intimidating. It was enormous. In the smaller school where I came from there were only two African American kids in my class and maybe one or two Asian kids. In this high school, it was much more diverse. There were many African Americans, Hispanics, Asians, and other kids from various backgrounds and cultures. Once I adjusted, I realized that the other cultures intrigued me, and they do so to this day. Finding someone you knew in the halls was a mission because we only had three minutes between classes. Lots of people were pushy and arrogant and, of course, looked down on every freshman. In addition, I was also "Terry's little sister." Since my sister was a junior, all her friends would tease me relentlessly. My sister would join them in making fun of me. Perhaps it made her feel cool. I don't really know what she was thinking, as I don't have a younger sister. I started feeling paranoid about bumping into them in the halls. Going anywhere in the hallways was dreadful. With only a few friends, I aimed to stay low-key, under the radar, and I avoided drawing attention.

Finding my old friends in those hallways was challenging. I started making friends with the people with lockers next to mine. They were friendly, and they admitted to being nervous too. I did see my old friends in the halls, sometimes in the same classes. There was so little time for socializing since we had only three minutes to stop at our lockers, switch books, and get to the next class. At first glance, there didn't seem to be any problem with my schedule. Algebra, Earth Science, World History, and Health. Wait a minute... Health? Nobody mentioned we'd have health class in high school. I wasn't keen on or comfortable being with the same loud and ignorant people from the hallways. I knew I couldn't avoid it, but I was still scared and nervous. Most of the guys in my classes were intimidating, so I steered clear of them whenever I could.

Health class wasn't a total disaster. When I first attended the class, the teacher was in the front helping one of the female students settle in. I figured that she had broken her leg because she was in a wheelchair. Her hair was short, and it was this stunning copper, reddish auburn color. I had red hair too, but I thought hers was much prettier. She had one of those laughs, when you heard the joke, you weren't laughing at the joke, you were laughing at her laugh. It was very contagious.

This girl in the wheelchair from Health class would become one of my closest friends and have a great impact on my life. It was cool that her name was also Lisa. The Almighty definitely had this meeting planned, because it was no coincidence. He had to have been worried about me because I constantly checked things like my books, my book bag, and the s-p-e-l-l-i-n-g i-n m-y h-e-a-d w-a-s g-e-t-t-i-n-g w-o-r-s-e. I was so anxious that I guess I needed something or someone to reduce my stress. I can't remember exactly what I said to her when we first met, but we clicked immediately. She had a twin sister who was just as nice as she was. I spent most of my free time with them, and their house would be my haven for many years to come. When there was tension at home, I would escape to their house.

I am Catholic, and my confirmation was approaching. I had the opportunity to attend a three-day retreat at my church. I really wanted to go and begged Mom and Dad. I convinced them by saying that it was a religious event and that there would be plenty of adult chaperones, so there was nothing to be worried about. They agreed that it was a good opportunity for me to socialize. The event was approaching. I packed my pillow and sleeping bag, and off I went. My dad drove me to the small school connected to the church. There were cars everywhere. A feeling of dread settled in my stomach, so I began counting the ceiling tiles in

the cafeteria, desperate to shake off the sensation of impending doom.

If I hadn't had all the ECT treatments, I could probably tell you how many ceiling tiles there were! I arrived and watched the teenagers in charge organize everyone into groups along with our belongings. Sleeping bags and pillows were scattered everywhere, along with large stuffed animals that I assumed belonged to the girls. After watching the activities for a while, I realized I might have judged these people too soon. They all appeared upbeat and friendly. It looked as if they were already having fun. I was welcomed by everyone with a hug and a, "So glad you decided to come!" These kids seemed sincere, not at all like the people I had met in high school.

There were various activities at the retreat, from older teenagers presenting talks on friendship, families, and prayer, to playing games called "icebreakers." These were games designed to help you get to know the other participants. They were usually very silly but always fun and lighthearted. I still remember one game where we all formed a huge circle. There must have been 60 of us! They passed around a roll of toilet paper, and each person was told to take as much as they wanted. It was a trick: we had to share one thing about ourselves for each square we took. I wasn't too thrilled about talking about myself in front of so many strangers, but I joined in. This retreat was my first of many. I had so much fun, and by the time I was a senior, I was the leader of the retreat, helping to organize the team and build camaraderie.

I made friends easily at the retreat because the other teens were similar to me. They accepted everyone regardless of background, appearance, or where they came from. We exchanged phone numbers at the end and started meeting every Friday. As we went through school, we became even closer. When I struggled with depression, these friends were there for me. I could call on them any time, day or night. Knowing I had them to rely on brought me comfort and relief.

All families have their difficulties, challenges, and triumphs. As I mentioned, I was very sensitive. I always tried not to say anything that would upset others. At home, there were often small arguments, whether it was between Mom and Dad or Terry and me. The big fights usually involved Terry and my parents. I wouldn't say that Terry was a delinquent, wild child, because she wasn't. She was funny and nice, but she tended to get into trouble. She wasn't particularly good at covering her tracks or hiding things. Whenever there was a disagreement at home, I'd escape to my bed to avoid hearing it. This strategic habit of mine continued into my marriage.

Usually, the arguments would revolve around my sister being her usual rebellious self, and Mom would step in with her mom duties, setting rules and boundaries.

My parents found it more difficult to maintain control over her. My sister didn't like it, and she made it apparent. I admired her in so many ways. She wasn't frightened to try new things and didn't appear to worry about who may be offended by her actions. I can't tell you how many times I heard Mom say, "Just wait until your father comes home!" I believe every child heard their mother say that while growing up.

Back then, moms stayed at home with the kids while dads worked. The dads were the strict ones who disciplined us. These types of conflicts were common in many households, including ours. It took all my strength not to cry when this happened. My sister did her own thing. This didn't pave the way to a fun and thrilling adolescence for me. I constantly felt anxious and mildly nauseous. My stomach churned constantly, and I felt like I was walking on eggshells. I didn't want to say the wrong thing and cause a disagreement. Remarkably, I found great comfort with my new church friends. Back then, the phones were still connected and hung on the wall, usually in the kitchen. That is how old I am.

The trick was to reach the phone first and find some privacy. I usually sat under the dining room table for a bit of solitude or against the wall if the family was watching. For my 16th birthday I got a phone in my room, and I was excited about that. Mind you, not my own phone number, just an extension of the primary phone for the house. Back then, houses generally had just one phone.

Like many teenagers, I spent many nights chatting on the phone with my church friends. I started feeling so depressed because there was always so much conflict in my house. Looking back now, I realize it was just your normal teenage stuff. It affected me so much because I was the "sensitive one." I would spend half the night on the phone with my now-endeared friends from the retreat and my friend Lisa. They tried to talk me out of cutting myself. I never really understood the urge to self-harm until then. It's difficult to explain to someone who hasn't experienced such dangerously low self-esteem. The internal pain was intense, yet no one could see the turmoil and conflict raging in my mind. Every time there was any conflict around me, I would cut up my hands and other places where people couldn't notice.

"There are wounds that never show on the body that are
deeper and more hurtful than anything that bleeds."
~Laurell Hamilton

I never really shared this with anyone, so many would find it surprising. Now, it seems strange and absurd that someone would even consider hurting themselves like that. The reasons were neither clear nor explicable. I was an excessively anxious and sensitive person, feeling things much more intensely than the average kid. I felt an indescribable pain in my heart that no one could possibly understand. I suppose it's because all my pain was internal, invisible to the outside world. I mostly cut my hands. The wounds were largely superficial, but there were times when they were more serious. It wasn't a way to get attention because I mostly did it in a way that others couldn't see it. It's one thing to notice someone with a broken leg; it's another to recognize someone's depression.

All of my self-hatred was contained in that blade. Ironically, it made me feel calm, almost like things didn't feel as bad as they were. Later in my life those self-harming feelings developed into thoughts and desires for death. Cutting was just a temporary band-aid and relief. The serious suicidal thoughts started later. My stomach was constantly in knots because of my anxiety. I was always in pain. This distress almost naturally led to the development of an eating disorder. I never wanted to become anorexic; no one does. However, the stress I experienced seemed to lead me down that path. I vividly recall hearing others comment on how fat a girl was or criticize another for lacking self-control, saying that's why she was so big.

I didn't want to be out of control. It was the obsessive-compulsive disorder that made me want to have complete control over everything around me, but especially in my body and my mind. How could I eat with my stomach always in knots? How could I eat while I was completely depressed? Soon people were commenting on how good I looked, "Did you lose some weight? You look great!" I didn't know it at the time, but this was positive reinforcement – something I actually remember learning about in Psychology 101. I was getting lots of positive feedback and compliments. I had nice, supportive, and fun friends from church. I felt skinny, and that boosted my self-esteem. My social life also increased.

After a while, it became harder to lose weight. I was desperate to get that positive reinforcement back, so I took a chance and hoped that those diet pills they advertised on TV would be able to work some magic. I also went as far as taking diuretics and laxatives. I was desperate for positive attention, control, and to feel good about myself when there were such negative things happening at home. One day I came home, and my mom was holding one of the boxes of pills. She said my grandmother had found them while cleaning my room. Strangely enough, my grandmother never went into our rooms. She only went to the main rooms, like the kitchen and the living room. I was mortified and devastated. Now my family knew my secret. The extreme pain in my stomach returned with a vengeance.

I felt so ashamed, embarrassed, and petrified of how my parents would react. They believed a psychologist would be the solution to my problem. I remember sitting in a dark office with an older, heavy-set woman. It's a vague memory, but it's there. This was my parents' response to finding those pills. They wanted me to talk to the psychologist about my feelings and "get to the root" of my problems. I remember sitting across the desk from her in a dark room. The chair was so tiny that I could barely see over the top of the desk. She was fond of playing games, which struck me as unusual for someone her age. As we played, she would try to make conversation, asking me questions about my feelings on various topics.

We even played pick-up sticks, a game I doubt many people know of today. For those unfamiliar, pick-up sticks involved taking turns trying to pick up individual sticks without disturbing the others. Imagine that. I couldn't fathom how this would help me with my psychological problems or make me feel better. I didn't understand what my parents thought this lady could do for me. She seemed like she was 100 years old, and she obviously knew nothing about weight loss since she was so heavy. Nonetheless, I played along and maintained a good front. Aware that anything I said would likely reach my parents, I was cautious with every word.

> *"Depression begins with disappointment.*
> *When disappointment festers in our soul,*
> *it leads to discouragement." ~Joyce Meyer*

Life and high school carried on like this for a while. I continued seeing the old lady psychologist and pretended to be happy, stable, and well adjusted. As far as I could tell, my parents seemed to believe it. As I entered my senior year, everyone was exploring different colleges and discussing their future fields of study. Senior year seemed to fly by with honor society inductions, SAT tests, the high school musical, yearbook signings, and, finally, graduation.

Perhaps the butterfly
is proof that you can go
through a great deal of
darkness and still become
something beautiful.

-Beau Taplin

Campus Confessions: The Monster in the Mirror Obscuring My Best Years

I had dreamed of going to college for years! Like any typical teenager, I longed to leave home. College was my chance to be myself, do my own thing, to pursue my own path, and to start fresh. The hot and sweltering summer after my high school graduation was filled with many shopping trips to get school supplies, bedding, cool posters for the walls, a small fridge, and a hot pot. It was a very exciting time in my life. My daily activity of visiting the mailbox gave me so much joy. I was searching through the mail to find letters from colleges trying to lure me to their campus. This boosted my self-esteem. I received many acceptance letters, and I felt this unbelievable sense of pride, accomplishment, and purpose. Many colleges actually accepted me, and some even granted me scholarships to come to their schools.

Despite receiving acceptance letters from all of the schools I applied to, my parents wanted me to attend a state school nearby. My sister had experienced difficulties being three hours away from home, so my parents set a two-hour driving limit for me. I was accepted to three state schools and one Catholic school in Pennsylvania, exactly two hours away, which I eventually fell in love with. I felt like I belonged there. The other schools were much larger and overwhelming, but this one was smaller, offering more opportunities to make friends. A smaller setting suited me better because large numbers of people increased my anxiety.

The day I left for college, I packed the car to the brim, pushing everything in as far as it would go, since my parents had no intention of making multiple trips. We drove a burgundy Ford Taurus with dark fabric seats and cruise control, a feature my dad loved, and I thought was pretty cool too. I have a fond memory of that drive. About halfway there, Billy Joel's 1978 hit *My Life* played on the radio. I belted out the lyrics with all the excitement that I felt in my heart:

"I don't need you to worry 'cause I'm alright,
I don't want you to tell me it's time to come home,
I don't care what you say; this is my life,
Go ahead with your own life; leave me alone."

I was having a blast at that stage, unaware of how difficult it must have been for my mom. She never wanted me to go away to college because of "my problems." She was so worried about me. Dad convinced her that a fresh start would be good for me. Despite her feelings, she never let it show. She kept a brave face the whole time, expressing excitement for me and maintaining a strong front. Mom would continue to consistently put everyone else's feelings before her own to keep the family together. She came from a long line of strong, capable Italian women who would do anything for their children, and she continued with this tradition. Mom was the cornerstone of our family, consistently ready to make any sacrifice for our well-being.

As I matured and started my own family, I continually witnessed her selflessness and strength. I deeply admired her and aspired to be like her. She must have written to me every day, because there was always a letter or a card from her in my mailbox. I eagerly looked forward to checking my box for her messages. I don't

think she knows how wonderful it felt to receive those letters, even if they just said, "*I miss you.*"

I loved college and the independence it brought. I enjoyed having the freedom and ability to choose what I wanted to do, what to study, and how to plan my life's direction. I was involved in many activities and did volunteer work, too. I signed up for the "Adopt a Grandparent" program where college students were paired with the elderly in a community who lived alone and felt isolated. This program aimed to help them with their feelings of loneliness and depression. This resonated with me because I understood the feelings of sadness and depression. As a volunteer, I found that this program was the perfect fit for me.

The weight of my depression and sadness followed me everywhere like a shadow, accompanying me even to college. The depression manifested in various ways, such as taking long naps in the middle of the day, insomnia, and a constant upset stomach. The stomach distress triggered the resurgence and worsening of my eating disorder. Gradually, the deep, horrible pain in my stomach led me to restrict my eating once again. Amidst all of this, there were many assignments due and papers to complete.

I spent hours doing research in the library and in study groups for the harder classes. The longer I was at college, the more stress I experienced. However, the people around me didn't know this. They couldn't see it because I hid it well by always wearing my happy face wherever I went. My grades were also always stellar because of the amount of time I spent studying. I began interacting socially with individuals and groups who shared my interests. I became a member of the Spanish club, and together we organized events and fund-raisers to support the local migrant farm workers. We even had mass in one of their barns, as I recall, and we sang the entire service in Spanish. Definitely something I didn't think I was capable of.

I continued to be really involved in Campus Ministry, where I wrote for the monthly newsletter and volunteered for different activities. My most enjoyable activity was singing in the choir. The other members were so much fun and reminded me of my friends from the retreat back home. Ever since the retreats, I had always wanted to learn to play the guitar. We did a lot of singing, and there were usually a few people who played guitar. I tried to learn, but I just couldn't figure it out. Having played piano growing up, I thought that would make it easier to learn the chords on the guitar, but I wasn't successful.

Mom and Dad always sounded upbeat when we talked on the phone. I told them I was trying a new instrument, and I think they were happy I was fitting in. After trying everything to learn the chords, I gave up on the guitar, even though I loved its sound. For Christmas that year, my parents bought me a new six-string guitar! I didn't have the heart to tell them that I had given up on learning to play. Because they believed in me and were so excited for me, I really worked extra hard to learn the chords. At last, I succeeded, and the first song I ever played was *Leaving on a Jet Plane* by John Denver. Don't be too impressed… the entire song consists of just three chords.

I eventually started playing the guitar at church and on various retreats. I played for many years of my life. A few years after the shock therapy, I picked up my guitar and tried to play like before. I even joined the folk group at church. I tried desperately to play like I used to, but I just didn't have enough coordination to play. I even found it hard to remember and re-learn the chords.

I liked my roommate, especially that she lived nearby and went home every weekend. That suited me because I didn't really like the party scene and preferred to hang out in the dorm and our room over weekends. My boyfriend at the time wanted to go to a big party, and while I wasn't very excited about it, I was okay with him going. Normally, we would spend our Friday or Saturday nights going to the movies or hanging out at a friend's house. I really hated the smell and taste of beer (and still do), so my boyfriend usually just hung out with me. In the dorms, the guys had to be out of the women's dorm by 10:00 or 11:00 p.m. Around 10:00, my horribly drunk boyfriend showed up at my door. Since I wasn't into parties and he didn't go to them often, he didn't know his limits and couldn't handle his liquor when he did. He came into my room and promptly threw up all over my floor.

I was only a first-year student and had no idea what to do with him and the situation. I frantically ran to get a friend to help me because I was dumbfounded. She came to help and was shocked. We decided to get our wits about ourselves. We had to make sure that the Resident Assistant on duty didn't find out; otherwise, my boyfriend (and possibly me) would get written up and have to pay a fine. One of the girls went ahead and called some guys to come over and get my boyfriend out of my room before the Resident Assistant found him in my room. The others helped me clean up his mess so it wouldn't smell so horrible when my roommate returned the next day.

My boyfriend was immature, but we had a lot of fun together. He always made me laugh and tried to help me be less serious. He was very insistent on repeatedly telling me that I was too skinny. At one stage, we were hanging out in his dorm room, and he put his hands around my waist. His fingers could wrap around my waist and touch on both sides. He would say, "This is not normal; you are too thin." He often said he should not be able to see all my ribs. We argued about the topic for months, but I was adamant that it was not an issue and that he should just drop the subject. I wouldn't listen to him. Every time he said I was too thin, I just ignored it. I was thin, just like the world wanted me to be. I hated looking in the mirror and would only look at my face, avoiding the rest of my body. I despised seeing my reflection and looking at myself in pictures.

Every time I looked at a photo, I would scrutinize it for signs of my fat stomach. This habit persists to this day, as I still judge my physical appearance in pictures. My current running group loves to take silly photos after our runs and races. While everyone else always looks great, all I can see in my own image is how fat I look. An eating disorder affects not just your body but also your mind and how you perceive yourself. Just because someone no longer looks skeletal doesn't mean the harmful thoughts have disappeared. It reminds me of an uncle I was very close to. We saw him frequently since he lived in New

York, just an hour away from us. He often offered me money to gain weight, which I found unbelievable at the time. Reflecting on it now, I realize I never did get that money.

Each fall, the school hosted Parent's Weekend. My mom and dad visited me, and I showed them around the campus and told them all about my classes, friends, and activities at Campus Ministry. The weekend ended with a formal dinner and dance for the students and their parents. Dad and I danced the night away! We were on the dance floor the entire time, and I was in my element. He was such an amazing dancer and had taught Terry and me to dance with him as soon as we were able to walk. Mom and Dad headed home the next day. I thought we had a great weekend together, but later that evening, my dad phoned me and asked, "What happened? When did you lose all that weight? ... You look terrible!" I was devastated. I didn't know how to respond.

I had no idea that my physical appearance would generate such a reaction from my dad. I thought I was just slightly too skinny. My dad further commented on how little I ate all weekend and how skinny I had become. Well, that was an awful way to end a great weekend. My parents continued by saying I looked so unhealthy and that I definitely needed help again. After their rant,

I agreed to go to one of the school counselors, but that wasn't of much help. Mom and Dad and I had many strained conversations on the phone, talking about how I was doing and how things were going with the therapist I had found.

The following journal entry from April 1992 was from one of those conversations:

Journal Entry: Dad's attitude on the phone this time was different than all the others. He was sincere, and he mentioned family counseling. I was surprised when I heard him say it because I thought he was against it. He said that he had hoped that college would snap me out of it, but I told him that people don't just "snap out of it." Maybe all of us together might work. Nothing is going to change if it's just me. I don't know what to think. I know nothing about this is going to be easy.

On spring break, my parents took me for a drive. It ended at a mental hospital that had its own Eating Disorder Unit. *Oh, good Lord*, I thought. *This was it; this was what they called "an intervention."* I knew what that meant. There was a man who "welcomed" me and mostly talked about the unit and that its main goal was to teach us that food is not the enemy. They would also show me healthier ways to eat. They had art groups and therapy groups to facilitate talking about our problems. He assured me that I would make lots of friends there. All of this made me cringe and roll my eyes.

However, it didn't matter how I felt because there was an ultimatum. If I did not agree to admit myself at the end of the semester, my parents would pull me out of school altogether. I reluctantly agreed that, at the end of the semester, I would admit myself to the Eating Disorder Unit. After finals that May, I went home and packed a bag with toiletries and comfortable clothes. I remember that morning I read one of those daily inspirational books. The "inspiration" of that day was, coincidentally, "Insanity is the act of doing the same things day after day, expecting different results." I cringed; this solidified it. I knew this would be no picnic.

I was extremely nervous and scared. I had no idea what to expect, and I was afraid I wouldn't make it back to college in August. Mom and Dad drove me to the hospital, and the admissions officer came to the lobby to escort me to my room. I don't even remember saying goodbye to my parents. I resented them for doing this to me. Why would they do this? I was getting good grades and truly blossoming in college. Mainly, I was doing so well because I was no longer living under their roof. Now I had no choice: either I submitted to this ridiculous incarceration or I couldn't return to school. I was desperate to get back to where I felt like my own person and somewhat in control. In reality, my disordered brain was far from under control, and I needed guidance to make healthier decisions and choices. From this point on, the decision was out of my hands, and I had no say in the matter.

A whirlwind of thoughts raced through my mind. Would they force me to eat? What would the other patients look like? I imagined they were skinnier than me, yet I secretly wished I were skinnier than them. I always wanted to be the skinniest. The double doors opened, and we stepped into the unit. They locked the doors behind us, probably to keep us "crazies" from escaping. Smart strategy, since all of us would rather be anywhere else. How would I ever face my friends again? This wouldn't be my last time in a psych ward, but that's a story for later.

Journal Entry: The Eating Disorder unit hallway was long and wide. It was decorated for summertime with pictures of beach balls and the sun coming down from the ceiling. The walk to the nurses' station seemed like it took forever. There were two nurses at the desk. They both welcomed me and told me not to be nervous, that I would be ok and that I would like the other patients.

How did my parents know I would be okay? Had they ever experienced an Eating Disorder Unit before? They were probably in their 50s and had obviously never been in such a unit themselves, given their size. At least I was thinner than those two ladies at the desk. My eating disorder completely distorted my thinking. Normally, I would never think that way about anyone, but the disorder turned me into someone I wasn't. I was taken to my room. There were two extremely low beds in each room. The beds looked like they were resting on the floor. I had never seen beds so low before. There was one big closet that had drawers for each of us to store our things. I would later use that closet to do hundreds of sit-ups in the middle of the night when the staff was not watching.

Later on, the day of my admission, my roommate explained that everything was arranged like this to prevent us from "hurting" ourselves or hiding anything. The idea of this hiding "game" sounded intriguing enough to distract me from what was really happening to me. She said that every so often the staff would "toss" the rooms while we were in a group to make sure we didn't have anything that wasn't allowed. They would basically take all of our belongings from us, and we would have to ask for them when needed. I experienced this when the nurse started unpacking my clothes. I was so shocked and felt violated. Wasn't there any privacy? They took inventory of my belongings and wrote the contents of my bag on my chart. Then she took me into the bathroom to do a "body check."

I was scared and expected the worst; I knew that I wasn't going to like what was going to happen at all. They made me undress so they could take notes of any bruises and the marks on my skin. They were also checking for razor blades or anything I could use to cut or harm myself. They also checked for drug possession. I felt so ashamed, exposed, and violated. I was stripped of everything, my clothes, my belongings, my comfort, my dignity, my self-esteem, and my identity. After logging everything, we returned to the nurses' station. I sat in a chair opposite the nurses' station while they went about their business, performing all kinds of administrative tasks. My greatest fear still lay ahead: They wheeled out a full-size scale. Oh my God! I stubbornly thought to myself that if they expected me to get on that monstrosity, they had better put on their fighting gloves because I would put up a hefty fight.

They tried everything to coax me into getting on the scale. When I refused, they stooped so low as to pull the "don't you want to go back to college" card. Those assholes! I already hated them. Feeling forced and without any choices, I got on the wretched scale. They made me turn around so I couldn't see my weight. Later in life, I continued to use that strategy every time I went to a doctor's office. People who don't suffer from eating disorders often fail to understand what it's like. We obsess over the numbers, haunted by our weight, until we can decrease it. We employ all kinds of methods to lower the number on the scale, exercising excessively and restricting our eating until that number is slightly lower than the last. It feels like a relentless game, a challenge where the number is never low enough.

The most terrible thing for me would be if my weight increased. It felt like the doctor and my family wanted to make me suffer by making me obese. My dilemma was that if I didn't gain weight, they wouldn't let me go back to college, the place where I truly felt I belonged. At that moment, I realized I had gotten myself into a real pickle. After "checking in," they led me to the group room, a large, beautifully decorated room. There was a presenter standing up, making some kind of speech, while the patients were sitting on the couches and chairs. All of them looked about as thrilled as I was to be there. The group session concluded with everyone going around the room, introducing themselves, and reassuring me that everything would be okay and that we were all friends. Yes, "friends," I wanted to be skinnier than all of them!

It was mostly girls, some in their teens, some older. Seeing a boy there surprised me; I had always thought eating disorders were only an issue for girls. Clearly, I was wrong. I also recall an older woman, likely in her 40s, who was extremely large. I struggled to look at her, and just seeing her made me want to lose weight. I hated how my brain was conditioned to think about others this way. Instead of wanting to know them as individuals, all I could focus on was whether they were skinnier than me. My thoughts had become deeply distorted.

Mealtimes were interesting events. We all gathered around a large table, expecting the worst. Fearing what would be served. Hospital trays were placed in front of us, all catered to us individually. It totally freaked me out just looking at it. Each meal consisted of a drink, bread, some kind of meat or protein, vegetables, and a dessert. If they thought I was going to eat that dessert, they were just deceiving themselves. The weirdest thing happened when we were done eating. The staff inspected everyone's plates and recorded the amount of food consumed. Additionally, we couldn't return to our rooms for an entire hour after eating. This rule was in place to prevent those suffering from bulimia from purging. Many of the anorexic people were also bulimic. I had resorted to vomiting only when I was truly desperate. Now, I was desperate again, but I felt like a prisoner.

Journal Entry: *"Dinner was gross. I cannot believe the number of calories these people are on. I can't imagine consuming that many calories and not being able to exercise. One of the girls told me that if I do not eat, they will put a tube in me. I can't imagine eating everything they put on my tray. God, I am so scared. Every time I eat, I feel it going straight to my hips. I am so fat."*

There were many "art therapy" groups where we used markers or pastels to draw. Sometimes, we had themes like "draw your best accomplishment" to boost our self-esteem or "draw your worst nightmare." Other times, it was simply coloring books and word puzzles, giving us a break from the constant focus on analyzing our minds while our bodies grew heavier. After a while, a few of the "inmates" began discussing their medications and the side effects they were experiencing. Others shared how much better they were feeling. I hadn't really focused on being depressed because I was so obsessed with my weight.

During my individual sessions with the therapist, she observed that I seemed depressed. We discussed many topics, but the issue of my depression became increasingly clear. In one of the sessions, I told the therapist the story of my grandpa. Earlier that year, my grandfather had passed away. I was remarkably close to him. My grandparents, my dad's parents, lived in Florida. They had spent their entire lives in Manhattan, New York, but when Grandpa retired, they moved to Florida. When I heard Grandpa was in the hospital and not doing well, I flew down to see him. The entire family was by his bedside, and I was unprepared for what I saw. I hadn't even considered how bad he would look, and just thinking about it broke my heart. We stayed by his side in shifts. I took the night shift with my dad and aunt, spending 12 hours at a time watching him suffer. He had been an alcoholic for most of his life, and it was finally catching up with him. The day shift was covered by my sister, my mom, and another aunt who was a nurse. Grandpa kept begging her to "do something."

I wasn't entirely sure what "do something" meant to him. I had the eerie feeling that he wanted us to put him out of his misery. I thought that sort of thing was illegal. When he started making the sign of the cross repeatedly, I became terrified that he was going to die right there in front of me. I desperately wanted to get out of that room. I had never seen anyone die before, and I wasn't prepared for it now. I asked my dad if he could send me back to college, but he said if I left, I wouldn't be able to return for the funeral. I decided that would be better, as I couldn't endure the thought of losing my grandfather and then being there for the final farewell. It would break me.

One of the hardest things I've ever had to do was say goodbye to him for the last time. I couldn't bring myself to say the actual word "goodbye," and it felt too final. I leaned in close to him on the bed and whispered in his ear how much I loved him and that I had to go back to college. Even though I knew he understood he was dying, I couldn't tell him it was okay to go. I wasn't mature enough to grasp anything about death, which is why I decided to return to school. It's also an interesting fact that later in my career I worked in a hospice agency whose primary goal was to make patients and their families comfortable, pain-free, and at peace with the impending death. Interesting how things in life bring you to places you never thought possible.

I was depressed, though I didn't realize it at the time. I had never fully processed his death or how difficult it was for me to see him so sick and near the end. I had a very special bond with him, and since I was born, my grandpa always called me "Kelly." I never knew exactly why, but I went along with it. Later, my parents told me that Grandpa had wanted them to name me Kelly, but they chose Lisa instead. So, he decided to call me Kelly anyway. My affection for my grandpa, the way that I had lost him, and my grief left a lasting impression on my life. The therapist attentively listened to my story and realized that I definitely suffered from depression, just like everyone else at the Eating Disorder Unit. She informed the in-house doctor about my depression. He prescribed an antidepressant called Prozac. It was a common medicine, as it seemed like it was the most prescribed drug for people with eating disorders.

For some comic relief, I must comment on the appearance of the in-house medical doctor. I can't recall his real name, but every time I saw him, he looked just like a weasel. With those thick glasses perched way down on his nose, he peered at me over his eyeglasses like I'd committed a crime, squinting with his nearly closed eyes. If he'd had whiskers, he would have been the perfect weasel. Once, I accidentally called him Dr. Weasel. I don't think he was too fond of me after that! I gradually adapted to the unit's routine. Every morning followed the same pattern: we lined up, had our blood pressure and temperature taken, and then got weighed. This was the absolute worst part of the day for everyone. We tried to make light of it, but it truly was dreadful.

I recall many sad things that I experienced there. There was a young girl named Sandra who didn't speak any English. I felt so sorry for her. She wasn't gaining weight. In fact, she was losing it. They had to insert a feeding tube through her nose into her stomach to ensure she got the nutrition she needed until she could eat enough to gain weight on her own.

One day I hit my knee. Here is my journal entry from that day:

Journal Entry: I just met with the doctor because I banged my knee in the shower, and it hurts terribly. He doesn't want to do an x-ray because there is not enough skin on the bones, and he thinks the radiation might hurt me. Is that even possible that there isn't enough skin? Looks fat enough to me.

It's strange reflecting back on the journal entry. When the doctor said there wasn't enough skin to do an x-ray, things became real for me. Not having enough skin on my body? Maybe it was worse than I thought. The memory of one girl I met there, Jackie, still haunts me. She was tiny in stature and had these dark-rimmed glasses. Her clothes simply and sadly hung from her body. She was obviously terribly thin. She had the appearance of someone who was severely malnourished, like someone from a concentration camp. I thought she was about ten years old when I first met her, but something did not seem

right. She did not talk like a ten-year-old. She spoke very eloquently and had very mature answers to questions people asked her. She had a lot of wisdom to share with us about why we needed to start eating and how important it was to work toward our goals. There, they focused a lot on setting goals and taking "baby steps."

After talking to her for a while, she revealed that she was 32 years old. I was shocked. Because of the anorexia, she had stunted her growth and would probably be that size for the rest of her life if she survived. That conversation struck me. I just wanted to have a normal life and get back to college. I just wanted to be skinny. Maybe being skinny was not something I should have strived for. I didn't know the answers or what to strive for. I was so confused. I never felt comfortable in my own body and my own skin (which I apparently didn't have enough of). I found this journal entry:

Journal Entry: I feel so tired. My stomach hurts a lot, but I just got my period. I feel embarrassed asking for Kotex pads because it makes it sound like I am getting better. I did well with breakfast. It is hard to eat because I feel guilty if I do and guilty if I don't.

Transitioning to a "normal" person was quite challenging. I had to rely on others' perspectives about my appearance, as my own perception was clearly distorted. I began to listen to the members of the group. The daily groups provided us with a wealth of life skills. The counselors taught us how to be assertive instead of aggressive. We learned how to overtly express our feelings instead of internalizing them. We were taught to say, "I feel angry when you_____." Or "I feel uncomfortable when you _____." I gradually realized that anorexia had become my method of expressing my emotions. Whenever I felt angry at someone, I would simply stop eating. That type of mindset persisted for most of my life. Even now, when I eat, I still think about the calories and occasionally restrict myself. However, losing weight in my 50s is much harder than it was in my 20s. Back then, weight loss was so much easier, but now, not so much.

My weight continues to bother me every day. Just because I'm not 90 pounds anymore doesn't mean my current weight is acceptable to me. The issue appears when I feel depressed and instinctively start to limit my food. Even now, when winter comes and I have to wear jeans, the anxiety starts. I still feel fat and have to coach myself through it. The disordered thinking persists to this day. I run regularly, do ab workouts several times a week, and follow numerous exercise videos. Talking about it is more accepted now because I am no longer in the "danger zone" weight-wise.

I never asked to feel this way or live my life like this. I wanted to go out with friends, have fun, and not worry about my weight. Gradually, I began to take things seriously. I wanted to return to college, where I felt I truly belonged. I loved my studies and activities and aspired to be like the counselors who genuinely helped people get their lives in order. How could I do that if my own life was in disarray? I had to get better. Anorexia had completely distorted my thinking. I found this journal entry interesting:

Journal Entry: I feel like my hips are disappearing, and it makes me feel upset and frustrated that there is nothing I can do about it. I used to live for that feeling of being able to feel my bones stick out, but I also want my boyfriend to like my body and how it is changing.

When I eventually gained enough weight to be discharged, things were different. It was a struggle to eat with my family. I felt like they were watching every bite I took. They tried not to look so obvious, but I think they all wanted to know if this "two-month intervention" had a positive impact.

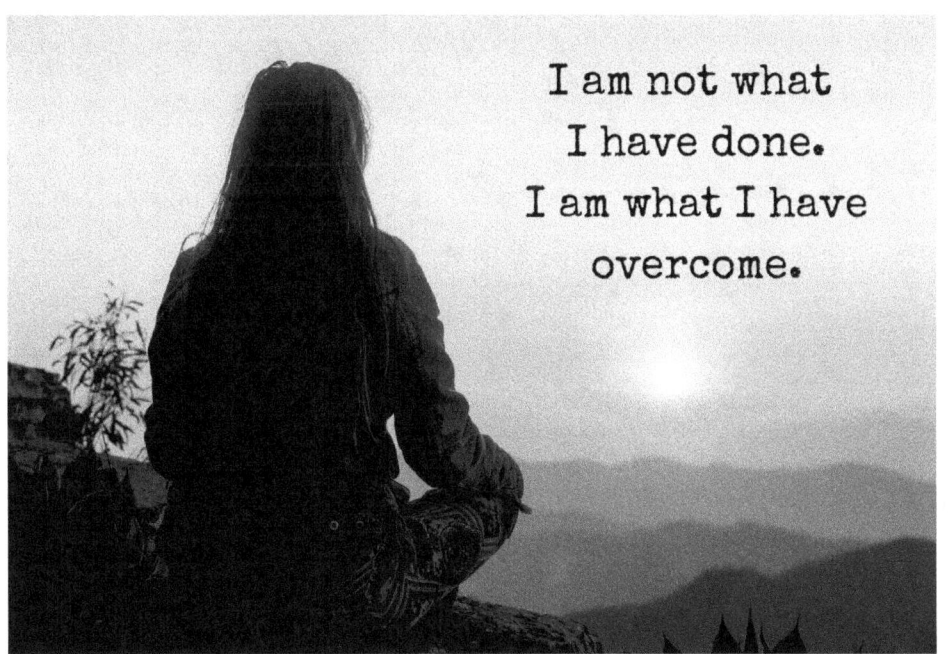

I am not what
I have done.
I am what I have
overcome.

From Disordered Appetite to Graduation: Stepping into My Healthy Future

I returned to school, and I had an incredible support system of friends. They stood with me in the food lines to help me get through the anxiety of dishing a healthy plate of food. This was significantly different from before the summer. Before summer break, my dinner was nothing more than a bowl of tomato wedges with low-fat Catalina dressing. That's all I ate for months. Now, however, I needed a well-balanced plate of food that any normal person would eat. Although I could never finish it all, I was at least making better choices. Despite striving for a healthy balance in my diet, I continued to keep a close eye on my weight. I also found a therapist in the area as well as a psychiatrist to monitor my medication and prescribe Prozac. I think people assumed that anti-depressants worked like magic pills. On the contrary, you had to put in a lot of work to make it work. I was scared to go back to school because I wasn't just going back to my old life in a dorm.

The college had appointed me as a Resident Assistant on one of the floors in the dorm. Being an Resident Assistant meant lots of training, being on duty certain nights of the week, being like a big sister to the women who were on my floor, and enforcing the rules. At that stage, I still struggled with healthy self-esteem, and I had all the added responsibilities. I resumed my studies and my activities at Campus Ministry. Things were going well. I continued playing the guitar at mass and found myself playing better than ever. I also noticed that guys started looking at me more when I was carrying my guitar case. It was like the effect of a guy carrying a puppy; it grabbed everyone's attention!

I also signed up for volunteer work at college, feeling it was my way of giving back. I resumed my volunteering with the Adopt a Grandparent program, now understanding more than ever the feelings of loneliness and sadness. I didn't want others to feel the way I did. Even though I felt broken, I wanted to be there for others experiencing similar emotions. The elderly in the nursing

home seemed to be just sitting there, waiting to die, with nothing to look forward to. Many had little or no family, so I made it a point to visit weekly. I loved listening to their stories of growing up and raising their children. It was so fascinating to hear about the types of work they did and the careers they had.

I visited this one woman regularly. She had been born with Cerebral Palsy. Her torso leaned to one side, while her legs leaned to the other side. She had spent her whole life in a wheelchair. When she was younger, her brothers and sisters would put her in one of those Little Red Wagons and pull her everywhere. She had been a permanent resident at the nursing home for years. Her speech was hard to decipher at first. It took a while to get used to the way she spoke. She had a profound sense of humor and loved it when I told her little stories and jokes. She had never gone to school because, back then, there were no programs for children like her. She couldn't even read.

I had an idea. I went to the local library and selected a few children's books that I thought she would be able to read and enjoy. We worked on the ABCs and numbers. She liked reading, even if it was just short and cute stories. We started reading a funny book about a little boy who kept causing a lot of trouble, but never on purpose. For example, someone would say to him, "Boy, are you in hot water!"

and he would take their words literally and retort with a funny comment that he just took a bath last night and he was perfectly clean. These simple stories and special moments brought lots of joy to us both. I think one thing my friend enjoyed was the time we spent together. At least for an hour or two, I was brightening up her day so she didn't have to feel as lonely and sad.

College offered a host of different experiences. I loved going to the athletic building to work on the machines, like treadmills and bikes. I especially enjoyed jogging with my headphones on, being free, and going wherever I pleased. Across the bridge, there was a beautiful park where cherry blossom trees came to life each year, painting the park in shades of pink, purple, and white. The playful barks of a variety of dogs filled the air, and I often saw tennis balls and Frisbees flying, with eager dogs leaping to catch them and return to their humans. I would find my running rhythm as I jogged along the dike that ran above the park and overlooked the entire park. My relaxed pace allowed me to enjoy the light breeze and warm sun on my face. The view was beautiful, and whenever I ran, I felt carefree. Despite managing anorexia and depression, jogging always lightened my mood. It also helped reduce my guilt about needing to eat.

Running and music were my main self-care activities in college. My guitar would go with me to my dorm and back to Campus Ministry daily. Then came a retreat for college-age students. It was held at a seminary that used half of the property for the seminarians and half for all kinds of retreats. Not only would I go on this retreat, but I would go on to be the student leader of the next one. As a student leader, I collaborated with the youth minister to select presenters to give talks at the retreats. We spent time reviewing the retreat plan and outline. I worked very closely with this gentleman, Paul.

Paul was funny, witty, and extremely respectful. It started to feel like I was laughing every time I was in his presence. I needed to laugh because I was always "too sensitive" and "too serious" around other people. Paul and I worked well together, complementing each other's strengths and weaknesses. He was 5'10" with hazel eyes and a flat-top haircut, and he always smelled good! I appreciated a man who took pride in being presentable and clean. We led the retreat and grew closer to a small group of college students who fit right in. Though we came from different colleges, we remained friends for many years to come.

Time flew by in college, and graduation arrived sooner than I expected. I had excelled in all my subjects and senior research projects, earning top marks, and I passed with flying colors. With a double major in Spanish and Psychology, I aspired to work in the fields of social services and mental health. I obviously had personal experience in these areas. I was excited about graduating but also sad to leave the place I had grown to love. Here, I was on my own and independent. Returning home would be a different challenge, but I would face that once I had officially become a "college graduate."

Graduation was a perfect experience. My parents were there, and my grandma came up from Florida just to see the ceremony. All the graduates wore their black robes, creating a unified sea of anticipation. In contrast, the professors' garb was a vibrant array of colors. Black and red caps paired with long black robes and gold ropes hung from their shoulders, while shades of purple and blue adorned their caps and hoods. I never really knew what a hood was or what it signified. It turns out they are worn by those who have advanced their education to include master's and doctoral programs. I remember wondering if I would earn such colorful hoods and ropes in my lifetime.

There was a whole gymnasium of knowledge and experiences that helped us graduates reach a goal that I, for one, never thought possible. This entire experience was much more colorful than I expected. Talking about the unexpected, my group of friends from the retreat also showed up to celebrate with me. I was so delighted to see them there. We all attended different colleges and universities, but our retreat had brought us closer, and we shared life experiences and achievements. I had not been expecting them, and I especially was not expecting Paul. I was thrilled that Paul had made the extra effort to be there. I graduated with a double major in Psychology and Spanish.

My degree would help me apply for and get appointed to jobs in addiction facilities, battered women's shelters, the county building of Social Services, and eventually the county nursing home, where I would go on to work with my most favorite population, the elderly. I was positive I would never graduate when I had to take the summer off to be in the Eating Disorder Unit. It was simply impossible for someone with this much baggage at such a young age to accomplish a college degree. Though my history was still a "secret," my new retreat friends knew about it and never disregarded me. They never gave me the impression that I wasn't capable of accomplishing anything so profoundly transformative.

When Paul, who eventually became my husband, began writing letters to me, he always described me as "capable." I had never been called that before. People would say I was nice, kind, and thoughtful, but never capable. That word still comforts me today. How did someone with such a complicated history of psychiatric struggles meet the challenge of graduating with a college degree? The journey was longer for me than for other graduates. Yes, there were the classes, the studies, and the finals, but I had to navigate all of it with a mind that saw things in a very distorted and unusual way. Each task tested my capabilities. With my low self-esteem, I doubted everything I had to work through. Paul highlighted even my smallest accomplishments, reinforcing the fact that I was more capable than I believed. That mindset continued to support me for many years to come.

I enjoyed graduation day with everyone dressed up and hundreds of people taking pictures of all the graduates. Unfortunately, this day was not just about celebration; it was about moving on to our futures. Our future already commenced with packing our belongings and moving out, usually back to our parents' homes. It was a short walk back to my dorm, which my family came in to see. I was staying in an all-women's dorm. It was a big old brick building with a second-floor balcony. My home for the past few years.

A hilarious story from that day always occurs to me. Apart from all the celebrations and that everything seemed to go well, when it was time for my family to return to their car, my grandma exclaimed in shock, "What is that awful, rancid smell?" It turned out they had parked near an old white Chevy S10 truck filled with cow manure. Who, in their right mind, would have a truckload of manure in the city at a university? Granted, it was a small city, but it was still a city, not the countryside where such things are common. To my horror, I later discovered that the truck belonged to Paul! I was mortified. The truck was deep brown with huge clumps of manure on the ground around it, and it was even dripping juices onto the pavement. My face turned darker than beet red. Over time, this story became a favorite to retell, always ending in hearty, roaring laughter and stitches in our sides from laughing so hard.

Later, after the humorous incident, Paul shared the story with me. He had been working in the garden and didn't have enough time to unload the truck. My graduation was so important to him that he showed up with a truck full of manure! I should have paid more attention to this incident, as this same lack of planning would persist for many years. Early in our relationship, we visited his mother's house. Her words still ring in my ears:

"Put on your running shoes now and keep running as far as you can!" In hindsight, it was good advice that I should have taken seriously. I also remember her describing Paul as a "bull in a china shop," an apt description. Every day of our marriage, he would come into the house like a whirlwind, immediately making his presence known with his clumsiness, many times breaking some of my best dishes and glasses.

I never craved for peace like I do now.
I don't wanna wake up angry, upset,
or have any negative thoughts.
I just want to be happy, and have
peace with everything.

Going the Distance: Marriage and Marathons

*P*aul and I officially started dating after I returned home from college. The challenge was that he lived in Pennsylvania, while I was in New Jersey with my parents. We talked on the phone daily and made time to see each other over the weekends. We both had jobs; I worked as a social worker at the county nursing home, while he worked for a company that operated group homes for adults with developmental disabilities. We both worked in the same field, which was good and bad. Good because we had that in common and each of us understood the many challenges that the other was experiencing; bad because neither of us earned decent salaries.

I mulled over the idea for a while before deciding to return to school for a master's degree in social work. It was well known that good money in this field was only attainable with a master's degree. Of course, it was never about the money for me; I chose this field fully aware that it wouldn't create a large amount of wealth. My aspiration was to become a private therapist one day. With my strong firsthand experiences, I knew the right things to do and say, as well as what pitfalls to avoid at all costs.

After doing some research, we found that a school near where Paul grew up had a Saturday MSW program. I worked my regular job at the nursing home during the day, went to my internship at a battered women's shelter at night, and drove to Pennsylvania on Saturdays for school. I would spend the entire day in classes and then later in the library doing research. It was very tiring driving back and forth. I was always a good driver and normally loved to drive, but sometimes I wondered how I got home alive with how sleepy I felt while driving home for two hours. I started to stop at Paul's mom's house after class to visit but also to take advantage of her comfortable couch. At that point, I think I could have slept on the floor if the couch wasn't available. It was also a great way to spend time with her and hear some of her stories of Paul's childhood.

Paul and I continued dating, and things quickly became serious. It didn't take long for me to realize that he was the man I wanted to marry. We had a lot of things in common; we each had experienced significant losses. He lost his father to lung cancer the same year I lost my grandfather. We often spoke about how our loved ones were watching over us from heaven, orchestrating our meeting long before it happened. It saddened me that I never got to meet the man who raised Paul. I would have loved to hear his stories about Paul, as they had been very close and spent a lot of family time together.

They shared a passion for hunting, spending countless days in the woods and in hideouts, waiting for the perfect moment. Hunting was a family tradition for Paul, involving not just his father and brothers but also many uncles and cousins. Paul has lots of hunting stories, which he shares non-stop. Paul's mother would often entertain me with stories of his childhood, emphasizing his mischievous nature. Her storytelling style was as fun and engaging as Paul's.

I was determined not to get married until I had acquired my master's degree. I knew many people who rushed into marriage before finishing their education and never completed their degrees. Often, starting a family took priority, and school was put on hold. For three long years, I commuted between New Jersey, where I worked during the week, and Pennsylvania, where I attended classes on the weekends. Every weekend, like clockwork, I would arrive at Paul's mother's house after classes and nap on her couch. This was a fantastic way to get to know my future mother-in-law! This also demonstrates how comfortable I felt in her home. She was very similar to my own mom, always prioritizing her children and joyfully helping with her grandchildren whenever needed. I graduated with my MSW in May 1999, and we got married that September.

Things were complicated with planning a wedding and finding a place to stay. Paul stayed in Milford, Pennsylvania, and we both liked the area. We found an apartment in an old farmhouse tucked away in the woods. It was an old and rickety blue house that had been converted into apartments. We found an apartment on the third floor because that was all they had available, and we needed a place that allowed dogs. Paul's beagle, Annie, was a sweet little dog with typical beagle hunting instincts. Whenever we were outside, she would catch a scent and follow it wherever it led her, which often made finding her a challenge. This turned out to be our method of meeting neighbors, as I would regularly walk around the neighborhood, introducing myself and asking if anyone had seen a little lemon beagle wandering around. Annie was a wonderful companion and loved going fishing with us. All Paul had to do was say, "Wanna go fishing?" and she would eagerly run and jump into the truck!

One advantage of living in Milford was its central location. It was the same distance from both of our parents, with Paul's mom an hour west and my family an hour east. I had always been close to my parents, and I know it was hard for them that I was so far away. Though they never said it, I'm sure they felt like Paul was taking me away from them. By choosing this location, we were trying to manage our new life financially, and it was more affordable to live in Pennsylvania where the cost of living was lower.

Financial considerations would become a recurrent theme in our lives. While we stayed in Milford, I started running again. We stayed near the Delaware Water Gap Recreation Area. This expansive park stretched for miles along the Delaware River, offering breathtaking scenery. Hundreds of tree species displayed a stunning array of green shades, transforming into a mesmerizing palette of yellows, reds, and oranges in the fall. The vibrant colors seemed to come straight out of a Robert Frost book, with every view worthy of a postcard. I loved getting back to running.

Living near the Delaware Water Gap Recreation Area provided many places to run and escape from the world. I always ran solo, never considering joining a group. Growing up with my dad, who was also a runner, I believed running was a solitary activity. I enjoyed having my music on and sometimes even danced to the beat while running. My sister Terry was known for dancing while running and it certainly made the monotonous activity more exciting. Some good 1950s music could easily get me through a six-mile run, keeping me engaged and entertained. I didn't care what people in passing cars thought of me, as long as I was having a good time. Running was always my break from "real life" and my way of dealing with stress.

Sharing a home with a man was a completely new experience for me, and it was challenging on many levels for years. My dad was a Marine, so we were accustomed to order. Everything had its designated place in the house, and we could always find what we needed because we were taught to put things back where they belonged. Now, I would look for a pair of scissors, and they wouldn't be there! Frequently, I wanted to strangle my new husband for making a mess in the kitchen. We had very different ways of doing things, so it was an adjustment that took a lot of time for both of us. Running became my way to step back and release my frustrations without taking them out on Paul.

My sister noticed that I had started running again and mentioned that she was also running. She told me about a race she and Dad were considering: the Rock and Roll Half Marathon held on Labor Day weekend at Virginia Beach. It sounded like a lot of fun! The description promised different bands at every mile, along with cheerleaders and plenty of spectators. This was all new to me, but I figured it would be a great experience, especially since the three of us would be doing it together. I had no idea how to train for a half marathon, so I bought a Jeff Galloway book on running. It included various training schedules and suggested working backward from race day to plan your regimen. Training in the Water Gap Recreation Area was challenging because most of it was flat, and there was no shade along the road. I got horrible sunburn that summer because I kept forgetting sunscreen. I still forget the sunscreen.

Race weekend arrived, and I was petrified but excited. The event was held at Virginia Beach, where the weather and scenery were perfect. The area was bustling with people and activities. There was a large Expo offering discounted running gear, from shoes to shirts and more. When it was time to line up, I was amazed by the sheer number of participants. There were thousands of people, more than I'd ever seen in one place! The big news of the day was alarming, and it was announced that we weren't allowed to go into the water to cool off after the race due to a recent shark attack. Good Lord, that's all I needed to hear! Before the race began, I noticed the extreme heat.

I had trained during the summer and was accustomed to high temperatures, but this was on another level entirely. Not knowing anything about the course turned out to be a blessing; it prevented me from obsessing over how I would reach the next water stop. Around mile 10 or 11, my knee gave out, and I struggled to keep up. Despite this setback, I was determined to finish the race, considering all the hours I had invested in training. Come hell or high water, I was going to cross that finish line. The race finished on the boardwalk, and it was quite a sight to see. The sun was beating down relentlessly, with no shade in sight! Positioned on the left side of the pack, I frequently stopped to grasp the railing, giving my aching knee a break and catching my breath. I repeated this several times just to keep up with my dad and sister. By then, my dad, a seasoned runner, had perfected his form, showing impeccable alignment and seemingly running without any discomfort.

Secretly, I felt a pang of agitation; here was my father, 30 years my senior, crossing the finish line effortlessly, easy and smooth, without even a hint of fatigue! Nonetheless, we all crossed the finish line together, which was truly exhilarating. We finished with a time of 2:24:11 and an average pace of 10:59. While I was thrilled, I also felt a bit disappointed, as it seemed we had been moving faster. Still, I was proud of our accomplishment. Little did I know back then that running would become an integral part of my life in the future.

A RUNNER'S *Prayer*

Run by my side;
live in my heartbeat;
give strength to my steps.
As the cold surrounds,
as the wind pushes me,
I know you surround me.
As the sun warms me,
I know you are touching me,
challenging me, loving me.
And so I give you this run.
Thank you for matching
my stride.

Amen.

Nurturing Lives: Pregnancy and Social Work

A couple of years into our marriage, I got a social worker position at a nearby hospital. At first, I loved it! It seemed like a small community, and everyone was very friendly. Sometimes a little too friendly. It was so small that everyone knew about everyone else's business, and it was common knowledge for all. I got the gist of how things went at my job and nothing else. Since it was a small hospital, I was the only social worker. I worked in the case management department. The department employed mostly nurses and was also supervised by a nurse. She didn't know much about social issues such as connecting people to community resources and helping people. Knowledge regarding these things is the foundation of social work.

Hospital social work had shifted focus from patient well-being to the financial "bottom line." For instance, a patient undergoing a hip replacement typically had an average hospital stay of three days. If the patient stayed longer than three days, the hospital would incur financial losses. The phrase "Length of Stay" will echo in my head for the rest of my life. The supervisor was highly efficient and skilled with numbers and statistics, particularly in monitoring each patient's "Length of Stay." Unbeknownst to the patients, the hospital meticulously tracked the duration of their stays, and it was my responsibility to hasten their discharge. This involved informing them of the need for a timely discharge while simultaneously providing counseling and connecting them with community services. This meant that I, the only social worker, handled getting them out of the hospital as soon as possible so we would not lose any more funds.

My supervisor often behaved awkwardly around others, and I suspected she had social anxiety. She would laugh inappropriately at jokes and interject odd comments during conversations. Working with her could be challenging, as she sometimes played mind games, saying one thing but meaning another. She had a habit of putting people down in a way that seemed like a joke, causing everyone to laugh, but I recognized it as manipulation. Having encountered similar behavior in previous jobs, I was familiar with her tactics. This became a significant source of stress for me. I just wanted to do my job and help people.

I excitedly shared the news that I was pregnant, and all the staff was thrilled. I loved being pregnant and feeling the movement of the tiny baby in my tummy. There are a lot of gaps in my memory during my pregnancy because of the many ECT treatments I had. I don't exactly remember the day that I found out I was pregnant, but I've kept the sonogram picture on my dresser to this day. I felt very hesitant about having to start wearing maternity clothes. I was not thrilled about gaining weight, but I was very dedicated to the health of the little one that would soon sleep soundly in my arms.

Our son decided that he was going to join the world two months prematurely. I blame this on a close family friend, Kipp, who had been out hunting with my husband and a few other men that day. They were hunting coyotes using foxhounds. When I was in the middle of doing my taxes from home, I got a call from the state police saying, "Ma'am, are you missing any dogs?" Since my husband was out hunting, I said it was possible. At that stage we were not using cell phones yet. The hunters only had walkie-talkies with them. The officer insisted I come and claim the dogs because they were running all over a major highway.

I politely explained that I was seven months pregnant and busy doing our taxes, but he wasn't interested in my protests. So, I got into our little blue Ford Escort and drove to the location the officer mentioned. By the time I arrived, my husband and his friends were already there. Our police officer friend, Kipp, was trying to smooth things over with the state trooper. The dogs had been in the back of the trooper's cruiser, which was now covered in mud and needed thorough cleaning. It became a running joke between Kipp and me that he was partly to blame for my water breaking two months early. The stress from losing the dogs and doing taxes was enough to push me into pre-term labor. After James was born, Kipp was the first of our friends to visit the hospital. He even brought James a stuffed foxhound for his incubator!

Our little bundle of joy was born in the middle of the night. When my water broke, I knew what was coming, but I had no idea how quickly it would happen! I assumed, since it was our first child, that I would be in labor for hours, just like my friends and family. But this baby had his own plan. He was stubborn then, and that trait carried into his adult life (don't get me started!). Our little one decided to come out feet first and got stuck! How on earth does a baby get stuck? Thankfully, the doctor knew exactly what to do because he could feel the baby's feet. The staff rushed me in for an emergency C-section, which I was hoping to avoid. I had dreamed of a birth like the ones on TV, where I could be awake and hold my newborn baby on my chest right after delivery. But that wasn't in the cards for me. They had to put me under anesthesia. My husband, who has always been squeamish about blood and bodily functions, stayed back in the corner during the procedure.

I remember waking up and hearing people around me, though my eyes were still closed. The nurse gently said, "Mrs. Conway, it's time to get up so you can meet your son!" It's a boy! We were old-fashioned and hadn't wanted to know the baby's gender beforehand. He was in the Neonatal Intensive Care Unit for seven days. Despite being born early, he was big for his age. We were expecting a three- or four-pound baby, but our little guy weighed a healthy five pounds! In a way, I was relieved. If he had gone to full term, he would have most definitely been a ten-pound baby! I'm quite sure my body would have suffered!

I loved being at home with my baby boy. I remember walking him up and down the street in his stroller, often stopping to chat with the older neighbors who were relaxing on their porches. They loved admiring him, and it was good for me to get out into the fresh air instead of staying inside all the time. Someone had gifted me a jogger stroller, so with plenty of time on my hands, I started going out for short runs with the baby. It felt so good to sweat and clear my mind of negative thoughts. Being at home day after day had its effects on me, and running was always my escape. It was my way of relieving stress, grounding myself, and gaining some much-needed perspective.

Things were going really well with our new family member for a while. I loved holding and cuddling him. I was on medical maternity leave, and I was able to stay home with the baby for a few months. We had our feeding and napping schedules. Everyone said that I was supposed to sleep when the baby slept, so that is what I did. Paul had gone back to work but was always thrilled to come home to his family and cuddle, love, and hold our son. We were a content and joyful family and thrilled to have a happy baby.

This is where my memory becomes hazy. I don't recall exactly how it happened, but I began feeling sad, withdrawn, and depressed. Despite having this beautiful baby boy in my arms, I couldn't understand why I felt so miserable. Everyone assured me that I was doing a great job and that we both looked happy and healthy, but I started to question my ability to properly care for him. I doubted everything I did. As the days passed, my uncertainty grew, and I often felt disappointed in myself. I began taking longer naps, and when Paul came home, he would take care of the baby while I went to bed early.

Don't forget,

while you're busy
doubting yourself,
someone else is
admiring your

strength.

Into the Darkness: A Visit to the Psychiatric Ward

Journal Entry (September 2003): I don't know what's happening to me. I love this little baby; he is my life. I just thought I would feel different. All of a sudden, I am responsible for this little person and I'm scared I'm going to do the wrong thing. Am I a bad mom? I just feel sad and a lot of times helpless. Is it supposed to be this way?

Paul and I were both aware of my long history of depression, but I don't think we realized it was happening again, or at least I didn't. Depression crept in like a snake, and I was so consumed by it that I didn't even recognize my own feelings. Yes, I was sad, but it took time for me to understand that the depression had returned. I had hoped that becoming a new mom would break the cycle of sadness and help me resume a normal life, but, instead, the familiar struggle began to reemerge.

It just got worse, and it became harder to hide it from the family. Mom and Dad would call, and I would have to change my tone of voice to be more upbeat and sound less burdened. I learned to cover things well and wear different masks.

> "It's not always the tears that measure the pain.
> Sometimes it's the smile we fake." ~Ritu Ghatourey

I did this while feeling terrible and horribly depressed. I stopped cleaning the house and washing the dishes. I couldn't scrape together the motivation and energy to do anything. I just spent time in bed.

> "Depression is like being in a totally round room
> and looking for a corner to sit in." ~Laura Sloate

One night, as the baby slept, I made the concrete decision to end my life. I had everything meticulously planned, but something kept nagging at me. I didn't want my husband or my baby to think it was their fault. It was all my fault. I was the one who was broken and introduced misery to the family. I didn't want my parents or Paul to blame themselves. This was my way of protecting them and securing their future. I knew this wasn't a one-time occurrence. My life was a cycle of getting depressed, withdrawing, and lying in bed for days before slowly emerging again. I didn't want them to endure this for the rest of their lives. I didn't want anyone to feel guilty. This was my decision and mine alone.

I remember writing letters to the baby and to Paul, explaining my thoughts about doing this. How desperately I wanted them to feel free from my mental illness so they did not have to deal with a life of misery. I was capable of handling my mental illness on my own, but I would never forgive myself for putting them through it. I was okay with taking the blame and going to hell if that was the trade-off for protecting my family against this illness. During the night, Paul realized what I was planning.

He lifted me from the floor, carried me to the car, and drove me to the hospital. They admitted us immediately. I guess it would have looked bad if they made me stay in the waiting room and then if I attempted suicide there. It would have been bad for their reputation. I put on one of those hospital gowns that was open at the back and got onto the stretcher. I couldn't understand why I had to wear the gown since my problem was mental and not physical. They took my medical history, and we told them about the medicine I was on and that I had been planning my suicide.

It felt like we had waited there for hours. I could feel everyone's eyes on me, as if they thought I was just another mental case. The staff just kept on walking by, as if I didn't exist. I felt humiliated, but I had no choice, I had to stay and wait. My husband was by my side the entire time. Eventually, a "delegate" came in. Initially, I thought she was a therapist, but she turned out to be an advocate, confirming that I was voluntarily admitting myself to the psychiatric hospital. My only reference for psychiatric hospitals was my experience in the Eating Disorder Unit, but I had a feeling this would be quite different.

They rolled my stretcher outside and into an ambulance. I felt so scared, alone, and ashamed. I remember the strong scent of antiseptics lingering in the air. I had no idea where they were taking me. My belongings, including the clothes and shoes I had worn to the hospital, were placed in a transparent plastic bag with white handles that snapped together. This bag accompanied me into the ambulance. They transported me to the admissions office of a hospital I had never heard of before. I don't understand why they subject you to such a complicated administrative process when you're admitted in that state of mind. I must have signed a stack of papers about an inch thick.

Most of the documents protected my privacy and were strictly confidential, which gave me a sense of reassurance. I didn't want anyone, especially my colleagues or my boss, to know that I was there or the reason for my visit. I started yawning uncontrollably. I realized it was the middle of the night. All the patients were asleep, and there was minimal staff around. They escorted me to my room and inventoried the few belongings I had brought. Then, to my surprise, they took my sneakers and removed the laces. What in the world were they doing? They explained that they had to remove any laces, strings from hoodies, or anything else I might use to harm myself. I thought to myself that people must get pretty desperate if they would use their shoelaces to hurt themselves.

After thinking about it, I realized it could be possible if you used the right "equipment." They said that my husband could bring me some clothes from home. In the middle of the night, the fun began as the process started. It was like my experience in the Eating Disorder Unit, but now I was a grown woman who had also recently given birth. The drafty hospital gown had to come off so they could scrutinize my body and record any scars, cuts, scratches, and bruises I had. Like in the Eating Disorder Unit, they were also looking for any weapons, blades, drugs, or anything that could be used to hurt myself or someone else. Once again, I felt like I was in jail and that the only thing missing was bars.

They gave me a pair of scrubs and those silly yellow hospital booties, then let me go to bed. My roommate was already sleeping. The room contained only two beds, each just a foot off the floor, with mattresses so thin I could feel the wood underneath. This was not going to be a pleasant experience. Exhausted, I fell asleep immediately. At 5:30 a.m., I was awakened by a woman who needed to draw my blood. To her credit, she was quick and found the vein on the first try, which was impressive because usually my veins go into hiding at the sight of needles.

The nurse came in and said my doctor was there, and he wanted to see me. I was confused. I thought to myself, "What doctor starts seeing patients at six in the morning?" Well, it turns out it was my very own familiar psychiatrist. I was in and out of this hospital for several years, and he was always there at 6:00 a.m. on the nose. It's as if my body was trained to get up that early because he came in daily. During my pregnancy, I only saw him a few times due to the medication I had to take. The risk to the baby was low, so we went ahead and continued the medicine throughout the pregnancy.

I went into a tiny office with the bare minimum, just a desk and two chairs. It was a dull and depressing room. The walls were a pale blue, and there was nothing on the walls. I sat down and stared at the floor. I felt so ashamed, and I felt like I had let him down in some way because of the suicide I was planning. He was professional but very personable and seemed to be genuinely interested in whether I was okay. He asked a lot of questions, and I mostly just gave one-word answers and stared at the floor. The topic of medicines came up, and he explained the medicines he was putting me on. I had never heard of it. We "chatted" for a few moments. He asked if I knew if there was a "trigger" to the depression. I wasn't quite sure what he meant. I just curled up on the chair and stared at the floor until our meeting was over and then I returned to my room.

A nurse woke me up an hour later again and instructed me to go to the nurse's station. There was a line of patients waiting to get their blood pressure and temperature checked, so I joined them. My eyes hurt from the bright lights, and I wished I could return to my bed to avoid talking to anyone. A girl named Marie introduced herself and reassured me that I would get used to the routine and should just follow what everyone else was doing. After that, I went back to bed. When they brought a breakfast tray, I refused. How could I eat? My stomach was in knots; I didn't know where I was or who anyone was around me, and all I wanted was to be home in my own bed.

My brain was fuzzy, and I was exhausted. Before Paul had taken me to the hospital, I had taken a large amount of Ativan. This was not to harm myself, but just enough to sleep through the entire ordeal. They told me to attend a group session in the "dayroom." I was so tired, there was no way they were getting me out of bed voluntarily. I don't remember how long I slept, but it was most of the day and part of the next. They brought my lunch and dinner trays to me, but I was more interested in pretending this was just a dream or an extremely horrible nightmare.

After a day or two in bed, they "strongly encouraged" me to get up and join the morning group. It was meant to help us check in with each other and see how everyone was feeling. The other patients seemed nice; they introduced themselves and offered to talk if I felt up to it. The woman leading the group asked each person the same questions: How did you sleep? How is your appetite? What is your goal for the day? My goal was probably just to get through the day.

They had groups on various topics such as self-esteem, anger management, a healthy diet, information on medications, and more on setting goals. I must admit that I really liked the art therapy group. We were given time to color in pictures, do word searches, and solve crossword puzzles. On other days, the therapist would ask us to draw a picture of how we were feeling or go through a long list of questions that we answered on our paper. These questions included our favorite kind of music, favorite movie, favorite snack, a one-word description of our personality, our hobbies, and more. This was her way of reminding us that we were more than our mental illness, more than the built-up sadness and despair. She helped us see that there was a real person beneath all the layers of self-doubt and hate.

In a way, it opened my eyes because I always felt like the withdrawn little girl huddled in the corner in the fetal position, all by herself. I began to like art therapy groups because it effectively reminded me of the good things in life. The hospital ward and rooms were all structured and planned well. The chairs in the dayroom were these huge, heavy plastic chairs that must have weighed 50 pounds each! It was hard just getting your arms around them. I figured they were like that so the patients couldn't get angry and pick one up and throw it at someone else.

The shower curtain had no rod, preventing anyone from using it to hang themselves, even with shoelaces.

The sink faucet was fully automatic, so nothing could be hung from there either. Even the garbage bags in the bathroom were brown paper instead of plastic, likely to prevent anyone from using them to suffocate themselves. This might sound extreme, but the reality was that we all had thoughts of death – our own death – constantly on our minds. We were desperate to end our suffering and relieve our families from it as well.

Journal Entry: What are we doing? Why am I not getting better? I thought this was supposed to work. I'm exhausted all the time, and my head hurts like it's being put into a vice and just squeezed hard. I hate this. I hate not being able to be happy. I hate that I have to put my family through this. This is what I wanted to avoid in the first place. I didn't want them to have to watch me as the depression just worsens. It's not fair to them. I feel so guilty.

There were lots of diverse kinds of patients. This unit was for the higher-functioning patients. Everyone was wearing either hospital scrubs or long baggy clothes. The people were black, white, Hispanic, older, younger, and from a variety of backgrounds. Depression certainly does not discriminate; I know that for sure.

During one of my later admissions, I remember working on a 3D puzzle in art therapy. I was making it for my son because he loved dinosaurs. I sat next to an older gentleman in his 60s who was very disheveled, with unshaved facial hair, and he never spoke in any of the groups. Somehow, it came up that he was a Vietnam veteran. I thanked him for his service to our country. He didn't say much, but I felt good knowing he had someone to talk to since I never saw him talking to any of the other patients. I asked if he wouldn't mind helping me with the puzzle since it was too much work for just one person. We worked on assembling it together and then painted it during the following art sessions.

Journal Entry: I don't know what I'm doing here. I'm totally depressed, and I'm painting in art class. How could this possibly help me? I guess it's better than some of the other groups they have here, where the other patients just bitch and moan about how bad this place is. I just want to go home and be with my baby. Why am I like this? What's wrong with me?

There were always outbursts and fights. During one of my admissions, a man actually managed to escape from the unit, providing the most excitement we had experienced in a long time. He had been acting very erratically, with his thoughts all over the place. To be honest, I suspect he had something like schizophrenia. The security measures were strict: for staff to move around the hospital from unit to unit, they had to touch their ID badge to a sensor on the wall near the door or elevator.

Patients were used to waiting at the double doors for meals, where the mental health technicians would unlock the door so we could walk to the elevator and go to the cafeteria. On one occasion, there had been a staff member coming into the unit, and this patient was so quick that he pulled her ID badge right off her and bolted. All the staff started running toward the door, and they called for some kind of CODE GREEN, or something to that effect. We all watched as the staff scurried down the hall to where he had escaped. We waited about two hours, and finally the guards brought him into the unit, and he was put in the "Isolation Room"!

The staff said he was finally caught a few streets away! I could not believe he had gotten that far; I was impressed! There was only one bed in the isolation room and no other furniture. The bed was so close to the floor that I think if he rolled over in a dream, he would simply roll onto the cold floor. He was yelling and screaming and disrupted the whole unit. We were fine with this. We

needed something to do other than color pictures. Hours later, after he calmed down, they let him out of isolation, and he rejoined the group. The next thing you know, he picked this huge picture frame off the wall and threw it across the hall. He even managed to put a hole in the wall! They finally had security come and calm him down and take him to another more appropriate unit so that the unit I was in wouldn't become so disrupted and upsetting.

After that incident, while standing in line by the double doors, I had the chance to examine the picture frames on the wall. They were firmly secured and didn't budge a centimeter, no matter how hard I tried to move them. This patient was incredibly strong in his agitated state, which really caught my attention. Perhaps "impressed" isn't the right word, as he certainly wasn't my idol, but he did manage to break through some of the unit's stringent precautions. So, kudos to him for that!

This hospital and unit became familiar places to me. It was like a vicious cycle. The first time I was there, they tried various medications, but to no avail. Nothing worked. I attended many group sessions, but I was still sleeping most of the time. I was just not escaping the depression and getting out of the hole, no matter what they tried and how many options they provided. I was still sad, depressed, and very withdrawn, not interacting much with the staff or other patients. I had taken medical leave from my job at the hospital, but we were uncertain about the duration of my absence.

Everything felt like a blur. I was so confused. As no other treatments were working, the psychiatrist suggested ECT, also known as shock therapy. I was genuinely surprised to learn that this treatment was still in use. My only knowledge of it came from the movie *One Flew Over the Cuckoo's Nest* with Jack Nicholson, which portrayed ECT as brutal and inhumane. In the film, the patient remained awake throughout the entire procedure, which involved electrocution.

It was terrible, concerning, and scary to think of this brutal type of treatment and that it would be done to me. We were told that it was now a much more humane way of doing things. They said it would be done in the hospital. I would be put under anesthesia, and I would be asleep the whole time. I wasn't aware of anyone who had undergone this type of procedure, so I didn't even have a reference or someone to ask advice from. The doctor said many times that it was "a safe and effective treatment for medication-resistant patients." It was a difficult decision to make, but the medications were not working, and we had to do something to get me out of the deep depression and back to my job. Our options were depleted.

When we asked the doctor about the risks, he mentioned that my short-term memory would be affected, but, with time, it would return. He also alluded to headaches that would follow "the procedure," but that those would be temporary. We decided to try it since my depression was so severe. They transferred me to another hospital where the procedure was performed. We were both scared and uncertain, but we were assured that this had helped a lot of people and that it was very safe. Our fears were eased, but we were not prepared for everything that followed.

Shocked into Reality

I am a person currently living with an active acquired traumatic brain injury, and I am authoring a book. That is a shock in itself. My good friend and running coach, Joe, nagged me for two years to draft my story, insisting that the public needs to know. Here we are 20 years later. I am afraid and anxious to share the next phase of my life, one of the darkest and most desperate periods I try to forget. I often turn to my family with questions about that time, as the many gaps in my memory leave me piecing together fragments to fully understand that part of my past.

The ECT therapy was described to me as your brain behaving "like a computer: sometimes you need to 'reboot' it to reset it." At that time, I was in a severely depressed state, extremely suicidal, and in desperate need of help to survive and care for my baby at home. Despite my depression, my husband and I discussed the treatment thoroughly and tried to research everything about ECT. Everything we found indicated that it was a "safe and effective treatment for severe depression." Further, we trusted my doctor, believing he had my best interests at heart. Only later did I discover how much money he, the anesthesiologist, and the hospital made from each treatment session.

ECT is typically administered in phases. In the initial week or weeks, patients usually receive three treatments, followed by two in the subsequent weeks, and then one treatment as needed in the final weeks. There is no standardized protocol for this; it varies based on the psychiatrist's assessment of what is sufficient. Interestingly, these procedures are not conducted by neurologists, who specialize in brain function but rather by psychiatrists, whose expertise lies in mental health and managing chemical imbalances with medication. At the time, we placed complete trust in my psychiatrist, not knowing to investigate the treatment and its consequences any further.

A typical ECT day would start with us arriving at the hospital at 6:30 a.m. We would take the elevator, and this usually turned out to be a nerve-wracking experience. The elevator felt ancient and shaky, turning each trip into a tense and anxious ride. When the doors finally opened, we would be at the nurses' station, where I would be admitted to the Short Procedure Unit. A nurse would lead us to a room, and I would change into one of those familiar, drafty hospital gowns. Then came the waiting for someone from the transport team to escort me to the Post-Anesthesia Care Unit, where patients recover from anesthesia. Despite so much being lost to memory, the faces of the two transporters are still vivid. One was an elderly gentleman who always made polite small talk during the ride. The other, a younger man, brought humor to the otherwise tense journey, making jokes to lighten the mood for both my husband and me.

As we passed the waiting room, I could see where my family would sit, anxiously awaiting word from the doctor that the procedure had gone well. My father often drove two hours early in the morning to take me to treatments when my husband couldn't be there because he had to work. Patients were required to have someone accompany them, as the aftereffects of anesthesia, such as slower reaction times and grogginess, made driving impossible. Once in the Post-Anesthesia Care Unit, I would be positioned with my stretcher against the wall,

and a nurse would come by to check my vitals and hook me up to a blood pressure monitor. Then, an IV needed to be inserted. This was a part of the process I dreaded every time due to my uncooperative veins. It often took three to five painful attempts to get the needle in, sometimes more, leaving me grimacing as they poked around and tried to find the right spot.

During one particularly harrowing session, they struggled so much to insert the IV that someone finally asked, "Can I put it in your foot?" That was the last straw. I demanded the doctor address this persistent IV problem once and for all. The solution was drastic: a doctor surgically inserted a tube into my chest to be used for all future treatments. This meant the tube had to remain in my chest for several months, requiring a home health nurse to come weekly to check it. After the ordeal of getting the IV in place, we were left waiting once more, watching as other ECT patients were wheeled in and connected to intimidating machinery. The sight of those connected to machines, their faces a mix of fear and resignation, added to the growing sense of dread that filled the room.

Journal Entry (October 2015): It's been a tough year. I went inpatient (again) in March followed by seven months of ECT treatments. Had a PICC line put into my left chest to make

IV access easier. I can't stand when they have to prick me over and over just to find a vein. It only makes the treatment worse. I hate this depression. It's not right that my family has to keep going through this. When will it end?

We waited interminably for the doctor's arrival, my anxiety mounting with each passing minute. In the meantime, his medical students would come by, placing electrodes on my head with a practiced detachment. I vividly remember them wheeling in the cart with "The Machine," a device that would devastate my life. It stripped me of my memories and forced me to abandon my career as a social worker, a role in which I had always been the helper, never the helpless. As a social worker, I was part of the team assisting families with various issues, from heating assistance to food banks, referrals to skilled nursing homes and generalized counseling. Never did I imagine I'd find myself on the receiving end of medical care, sitting on a cold, stiff stretcher under the scrutinizing eyes of the staff. I felt ashamed, vulnerable, and utterly defeated.

In the midst of my mental turmoil, the doctor would finally arrive, often with five other ECT patients waiting on stretchers. I always hoped to be first, to escape the torment of hearing the treatment being administered to others. Though they would close the curtain for privacy, the muffled conversations and final checks before the anesthesiologist pushed the medication were very audible. The dreaded "all clear" would echo through the room, signaling that "The Machine" was set to the voltage deemed appropriate.

If the treatments didn't yield the desired results, the doctor would decide whether to increase the voltage. This decision felt shrouded in mystery, with no apparent guidelines on settings, eligibility, or maximum limits. Unlike FDA-regulated medications, ECT guidelines are not standardized. I've often wondered what settings they used on me, especially as my treatments continued to escalate. After more than 100 sessions, the question of how much electricity was ultimately sent through my brain lingers, a haunting uncertainty.

As I lay there, electrodes being placed on my head by medical students, I couldn't help but fixate on the cart that held "The Machine," that life altering device, robbing me of memories and forcing me to abandon my career. The silence before the treatment felt like an eternity, broken only by a long, ominous beep. Afterward, there would be a brief exchange between the doctor and staff before they moved on to the next patient, wheeling "The Machine" to its next victim.

As I said earlier, the medical students would hook up the electrodes to my chest and head. I found it weird that they would just place them on my temples. I felt they placed the electrodes haphazardly, without referencing any brain map or personalized diagram of each person's individual brain. I mean, my brain shape and size could be different than the patient next to me. But that is exactly what they did. They had me take out any pins or metal hair clips, I guess because they would have an impact on the actual electricity that would be forced into my brain.

Then I have one truly clear memory of the doctor putting a wet sponge on my head before they were about to administer the treatment. He said that "water is a good conductor for the electricity." Immediately the movie *The Green Mile* would pop into my head. I thought about how the prisoners on death row would walk into the room where the electric chair was, and they would be strapped to the chair while the guards were strapping them down and placing the electrodes on them.

Before putting a metal bowl-like contraption on the man's head, they would place a wet sponge there below the contraption. Then they would put the bowl on his head and secure it in place. It was that bowl-like contraption that sent the electricity through their body. When I thought of this scene, I started feeling intensely ashamed and traumatized. It was as if I was being tortured, as if I was being electrocuted. But, truly, I *was* being electrocuted! After that, every time I went for a treatment, I felt like I was going to the gas chamber or the electric chair for my crimes. My crimes of being sad and depressed and just not normal to begin with.

How could this possibly be good for anyone? The only moment of relief came just before they placed the oxygen mask over my face, when that strange, euphoric feeling would wash over me as I drifted off to sleep. I clung to that moment, desperate to escape the voices hovering above me, as if I wasn't even there. One detail stands out with vivid clarity: each time before I was put under, my psychiatrist would hold my hand, offering a small but essential comfort. It was the reassurance I needed to surrender to the anesthesia and let the procedure unfold without resistance.

I always felt a genuine connection with my psychiatrist, believing he had my best interests at heart. But it wasn't until many years later that I began to piece together what had really happened. I hadn't revisited those days until now, as I write this book. For someone who suffered such severe memory loss, it's astonishing to recall so many details of those treatments. I wonder if these treatments and the harrowing experiences that came with them have also caused post-traumatic stress disorder.

I do not know how to feel right now, having just relived the terror of my past – the thing we would never talk about. The large, horrible elephant in the room. The thing that was right in front of our eyes, yet many things went unsaid. I never talked about my experience to my husband, my father, or the rest of my family. I mean, what good could come out of me sharing the horror of what was done to me? It would only serve to make them feel guilty for something they had no control over. None of us knew anything about what the long-term effects would be and how drastically they would change the rest of my life. Not even the consent form said anything about the long-term cognitive and neurological side effects of the treatments or that they could cause permanent brain damage. Not even the doctor said anything about the side effects that would never go away.

According to Irving M. Reti, M.B.B.S., the director of the Electroconvulsive Therapy Service at The Johns Hopkins Hospital, "some 100,000 Americans undergo ECT treatments each year." I just had to include this statistic to emphasize that this is still happening and that it is being done to many people. I should have sensed from the first mention of it that something was not right: "Convulsive Therapy." Convulsive therapy means they induce seizures, not just any seizure, but a grand mal

seizure. From what I know about people who suffer from epilepsy, they take strong medications to prevent seizures. So, if they are trying to prevent seizures, why would I let my doctor induce one? Not just one seizure, but 100+ seizures over the course of several years. How could I not realize this could only be harmful to my body? People who experience too many seizures, like those who suffer multiple concussions or brain injuries, are more likely to suffer neurological consequences and damage.

Before these treatments, I was highly successful and functional, but the ECT has impaired essential cognitive functions. I now struggle with word retrieval, spelling, and maintaining focus. I have difficulty with speech, often stuttering and finding it hard to articulate my thoughts. These issues become increasingly evident in my interactions with others. In the American medical field, a significant controversy surrounds the question of whether ECT causes brain damage. The psychiatric community staunchly maintains that ECT does not result in brain damage, citing longstanding research as evidence. However, this position relies heavily on older studies, often disregarding more recent findings.

Standard MRIs do not reveal ECT-related damage, which only becomes apparent with more advanced imaging techniques. Such damage occurs on a cellular level, a fact that many psychiatrists continue to deny. Consequently, they argue that the absence of evidence on traditional MRIs means there is no brain damage or injury. They assert that the machine they use does not indicate any risk of permanent damage to patients. Despite multiple patients experiencing all the symptoms of a brain injury, admitting that ECT causes cognitive side effects would subject medical professionals to intense scrutiny from the medical community.

As an ECT survivor, I have found that no neurologist is willing to treat me, instead referring me back to the psychiatrist responsible for my condition. If my psychiatrist acknowledged any form of damage, it could open the door to numerous legal cases from patients who suffered brain damage and other damages from these treatments. This is an ongoing struggle for those of us who have already suffered brain damage. We are unable to get help for our neurological problems because the medical community refuses to acknowledge the possibility of consequent brain damage.

"Insanity: Doing the same thing over and over again expecting different results." ~Albert Einstein

I used to worry
about tomorrow,
but that was before
I survived yesterday.
Now it's one breath
at a time.

-Alfa

Picking Up the Pieces of My Scattered Life: Navigating the Struggle to Reclaim Normalcy Post-ECT

We embarked on the treatments with nothing but a fragile hope that they might lift the weight of depression. While they did offer some respite, it was fleeting, and we found ourselves facing an unexpected journey of over 100 sessions. The long-term consequences were beyond anything we had imagined. Words began to elude me during conversations, and I developed such a severe stutter that I often abandoned speaking altogether to avoid the humiliation. The chronic migraines, sometimes occurring four or five times a week, took us all by surprise and drained my ability to function. My ability to think, reason, and communicate deteriorated, altering my interactions with the world around me. None of us foresaw that I would lose 15 years worth of memories, a significant portion of my life erased like chalk from a blackboard.

I couldn't recall significant parts of my life, such as my son's milestones and his first days of school. The memories of holidays, weddings, and even funerals had vanished, leaving me to constantly ask family members about various special occasions. "How was the wedding? Did Dad and I dance? Was my son surprised on Christmas Day when we bought him that cool remote-control car? What happened at my son's fifth birthday party; was I even there?" My husband would say I was physically present, but my mind was miles away, showing no emotions. I was never happy or interested in anything. I was absent-minded, making silly mistakes, and even my common sense seemed to have disappeared. I started hearing a maddening sound in my head. It was a constant buzzing that never goes away, sometimes growing louder as my headaches worsened.

The headaches and memory loss worsened until the depression reared its ugly head again, landing me back in the psych ward. They would "adjust" my medications, sometimes adding two or three more. I remember being on lithium and having such terrible tremors that I couldn't get the corn from my fork to my mouth without it falling off. Severe depression would start again at home over a few weeks or months, sending me back to the hospital. This was followed by a series of ECT treatments and several weeks out of work to let my brain regain its functioning. Returning to work was hard because I didn't want to lose my job, but I was rarely functioning at a level where I could be effective.

I had a fast-paced job, juggling a large caseload of patients. It often felt like I was juggling ten tasks at once, leaving me overwhelmed and drained of energy. I was expected to be a positive influence on my co-workers and especially on clients. I had to manage all this even when I had a night filled with nightmares that robbed me of quality sleep. The desperation for a 30 minute nap became overwhelming. I even sometimes considered sneaking into an office, locking the door, and taking a quick snooze. I did all of this and more just to keep functioning at work, let alone trying to do my job diligently and efficiently.

All the while, I had to conceal my mental health struggles out of fear that revealing them would cost me my job. I was in this threatening position countless times. I remember returning to work. At the time I was earning more money than Paul, and I felt the responsibility to get back because we had our normal bills and thousands of

dollars in medical expenses. The hospital and doctors didn't waste any time sending their bills. As mentioned before, I worked at a small hospital in a close-knit community. Everyone knew what was happening in everyone's lives; gossip was a common occurrence amongst staff. Returning to work felt like walking into the lion's den, with the lion standing there, mouth wide open and drool oozing out. I was in contact with my supervisor, and we agreed I would start by working three days a week. Paul's sister kindly offered to watch the baby, for which we were profoundly grateful.

When I saw my supervisor, there was no conversation about the hospital. There was just a cordial greeting and an update on current happenings. Everyone was amiable and nice, but it was very awkward. They didn't know what to say, though I knew they were dying to get some details about "the psych ward" and what had landed me there. Was it okay to say, "Are you feeling better?" This was fine with me. It was like they were unfamiliar with interacting with someone with mental illness. This was in a hospital, of all places.

My fellow employees didn't dare ask any specific questions. Most times, they would start by asking how my son was. I think they were secretly wondering how my family was coping with the chaos and confusion of feelings. They were probably hoping to get some "dirt" on what happened. I recall one of the worst days after I returned to work. I was behind the nurse's station. One of the doctors was sitting at the desk with his physician assistant, and he turned around and said to me, "Maybe they need to put you back in that hospital and adjust your meds!" I felt so embarrassed. There was a shocked silence. You could hear a pin drop. One of the nuns, also a dear friend of mine, came up behind me very quietly, gently took my hand, and led me down the hall to her office. I broke down and began sobbing terribly.

How could a physician of all people humiliate one of his co-workers like that? I never had any bad experiences with him previously, so I could not figure out exactly where that comment came from. One would think that in the medical community, professionals would be especially sensitive to one of their own having to go through what I went through. It was hard enough trying to function with a brain of mush and no memory, let alone deal appropriately with the hostility in a place that is supposed to be a place of healing.

That friend of mine stood by me through some of my worst days at work. I think about her often, especially when I am reading my entries from my journal that she most kindly gifted me. I wrote about most of my hospitalizations in that journal. The peculiar thing was that it was the only "notebook" the psych hospital would allow me to bring along when I was admitted because it did not have a wire binding or a ribbon to mark the pages, things that they considered could be a danger to me or someone else. The name of the journal is The Goddess Within. It is an empowering journal, helping women to find their own goodness and gifts. She was from another country and had a noticeable, beautiful accent. She was soft-spoken, but when she had something to say, she wasn't discreet, and she didn't count her words. She was most definitely a warrior and would defend her friends!

During all my years of employment, I only had one supervisor who stood by me, offering unwavering support and encouraging me to simply do my best. She never judged me or treated me differently, understanding that when I was at my best, I was enthusiastic, thorough, and dedicated to my work. I hope to always remember the kindness she showed me. If my mental illness or brain injury ever clouds that memory, at least it is now preserved in this book, ensuring it remains part of my story forever.

Lost in the Maze: Seeking Elusive Purpose Amid Repeated Psych Admissions

"That's the thing about depression: A human being can survive almost anything, as long as she sees the end in sight. But depression is so insidious, and it compounds daily, that it's impossible to ever see the end. The fog is like a cage without a key." ~Elizabeth Wurtzel

During most of my early hospitalizations, I was withdrawn and silent, barely interacting with anyone in the unit for days on end. However, during what I believe was one of my last stays, my demeanor shifted dramatically. Anger consumed me, and I flat-out refused to sign the papers for voluntary admission. This defiance landed me in the involuntary holding area until they could legally commit me for a minimum of three days. Once

admitted, my psychiatrist informed me that an involuntary commitment, known as a 302, would appear on my driving record. Faced with this revelation, I swiftly recanted and reluctantly signed the voluntary admission papers.

The staff this time around was quite different. Some of the familiar faces I had come to know well were still there. They were the dedicated mental health technicians who, despite being at the bottom of the totem pole, spent most of their time counseling us and running the groups. However, the new technicians were inexperienced and inattentive to our psychological needs. They never went out of their way to informally "check in" with us or strike up a conversation. Twice daily, our temperatures and blood pressures were taken: first thing in the morning and again in the evening. I found it peculiar that the technicians, not the actual nurses, were responsible for taking our vitals. This irked me to no end. Having worked on psych wards and in hospitals, I knew a fair amount about medical procedures. When a "young kid," barely in his 20s and clearly on his first real job, took my blood pressure and nonchalantly told me it was 150/90. I couldn't help but feel a surge of concern.

As a runner, my blood pressure was always low. So when this young technician casually said, "It's fine, next!" after recording 150/90, I was livid. That reading was high for anyone, but especially for me. The usually quiet, reserved redhead who kept to herself and never made waves suddenly put up a stink. Did he have any idea what a safe blood pressure was? Did he even ask if that was a high reading for me? Nope! So, I caused a big fuss and insisted that a nurse take my blood pressure properly with a stethoscope, not just rely on an automatic machine that little Johnny here could operate with the push of a button. By the time the nurse arrived, I was really worked up, so naturally, my blood pressure was still high. She suggested I walk the halls for a while to calm down, promising to recheck it later.

When it comes to walking the halls of a psych ward, one might imagine a highly regimented environment filled with groups, therapy sessions, medication management, and recreation. Bulletin boards plastered with the daily schedule and group activities give the impression of a structured routine. However, the reality was far less organized. They had groups, but they were rarely thoughtfully planned or mindfully put together by a social worker or therapist. In all my inpatient stays, I hardly recall any therapist running the groups. The exception was a lone psychiatrist who would conduct group therapy once a week; he seemed to be the only staff member who truly knew how to counsel anyone. Typically, these groups

were led by mental health technicians, who, despite their dedication, had the least amount of knowledge and training to run a proper session. Keep in mind that I had work experience in these fields and used to do this for a living. I knew what a well-run group and hospital were supposed to look like.

There was so much "down time" since the groups were very short and to the point. Most of us would just spend hours walking up and down the halls. I was always awake during the night. The night staff knew me well. I paced all night and then would try to go back to bed, but I was not sleepy, so I got up and kept walking. Walking and pacing were the only things to do unless we wanted to color. As in coloring with crayons...

Since there were really few organized groups or activities over weekends, we spent most of the day coloring pictures. These were all adults aged 18 and older, not little kids. I will say that the coloring could be relaxing once you got into it, but it was a little demeaning. Surely, they could provide more age-appropriate activities. They had some games, but they were locked up in a cabinet, and none of the staff ever knew where the key was. We played cards because that was the only alternative. I would sometimes join in, but only after I had been in the unit for a while. During the first week, I was always withdrawn, avoiding eye contact and not talking to anyone. The art therapist working at the hospital was there for all my admissions, over all those years. We engaged in various therapeutic activities, such as creating pictures to express our feelings. We drew, used pastels, and painted with watercolors to depict what was happening in our lives. She would also play the radio while we worked, which was a rare treat in a place where music was usually absent.

I was in a truly confused and desperate state at that stage. In one of the art sessions, the therapist asked us to draw a picture representing where we were in our recovery process. Each of us created something different. Some were happy pictures, others dark and gloomy. When it was my turn, my mind went completely blank. I couldn't comprehend how I had ended up back here, especially since I had been doing so much better at home. I was diligently following my psychiatrist's and therapist's advice, taking my meds, getting exercise, and maintaining a good diet. Yet, these episodes always seemed to come on so suddenly, leaving my brain in a dark place and me wanting to give up. I had no clue where I stood mentally. The only thing I could think to draw was a big black question mark. When it was time to explain our pictures, I couldn't find the words. Instead, I wept quietly and asked them to move on to the next person.

The art therapist knew me well from all my past admissions (20 or more...). After class, she asked me to stay behind for a chat. I broke down in her arms, weeping, as usual without clear reasons. So many questions flooded my mind. Why was I back here again when I was doing everything right at home? What more could I do to keep depression at bay? What could I have done differently to prevent another episode, despite doing everything right? My future loomed ahead like the vast black question mark I had drawn. I was filled with uncertainty and fear about the darkness that might lie ahead.

She tried to comfort me, reminding me of my "WHY." Everyone has a why, it was the reason for staying alive. It's the driving force that keeps us going, the reason we take our meds, the reason we fall and get back up to try again. After our conversation, I was tagged as a suicide precaution patient. This label was assigned to alert staff to be especially attentive and concerned about patients with thoughts of self-harm and suicide. As a suicide precaution patient, I was essentially confined to my room with a staff member present every minute of the day. Even when I needed to use the bathroom, I had to leave the door open so they could watch me.

Most times, it was a younger, inexperienced staff member sitting in an office chair in the doorway, absorbed in their iPhone rather than engaging in meaningful conversation or counseling. I was on suicide precaution multiple times throughout my hospitalizations. It was always the same: instead of addressing my emotions, I was confined and left alone with my thoughts, like a prisoner contemplating the crimes I had committed.

In these moments, my thoughts turned to my "WHY." My son has always been my reason to survive.

Journal Entry: I hate how it makes me look to my son. I must look shameful, like a horrible mom. I wonder if kids make fun of him because his mother is crazy. It breaks my heart that I can't be normal. I don't want him to have to live with this, but I just love him so much. I don't want to disappoint the family, but I don't know if I can keep on doing this. Going home, being ok for a few weeks or months and then all of a sudden, I'm in bed all day, and back to the hospital I go. I just can't keep doing this to them.

How does a child, growing up with a mother who was usually depressed or in the hospital, function normally? How do they have a normal upbringing? I'm sure his friends knew what was happening. We never kept it a secret from anyone. We were always incredibly open and honest about what I was going through. I can't imagine how my husband suffered every time I was readmitted to the hospital. How did he explain it? What did he say? *"Your mom wants to hurt herself so she will be safer for a while in the hospital."*?! How did he even begin to tell him about my illness, an illness that can't be seen or understood? How did he discuss this with our son when he was old enough to understand and reveal the truth about the reasons why someone goes to the psych hospital?

My son and I had a special connection, and we were always remarkably close. He sensed when I was not feeling well. He would spontaneously just come and wrap his arms around me and give me the biggest and tightest bear hug. He would do this even when he was incredibly young and even now while he is an adult. He was always my WHY. He was my reason to keep on trying. I wanted so desperately for him to have a strong woman as a mother, a mother he could always count on to be there to love him and support him no matter what the situation was. I remember the times I could talk to him on one of the few phones available for patients. He was always so calm, reassuring me that everything would be okay. He told me I needed to be in the hospital right now and promised to give me a huge hug once I was discharged.

Journal Entry: I just talked to James on the phone. He sounded so sad. I know he misses me. I can't imagine what it's like for Paul to have to tell him about all of this. What a horrible thing to have to talk to your child about. I tried to sound happy and positive on the phone, but as soon as the call ended, I couldn't stop crying. God, what am I doing? I'm ruining everyone's life and for what? Nothing. If I wasn't here then at least they wouldn't have to deal with this stupid revolving door of this stupid hospital. I hate this place! I'm so confused. God, please help me.

I felt guilty for many years, and I still do. I felt guilty for being so weak and absent. Yet, every time I'm with my son, I make a point to tell him that he is the best thing that ever happened to me. I tell him this repeatedly, always praising him for his strength and for loving me even when I wasn't feeling well. He has always been, and continues to be, the greatest gift I could ever have received. I want to make sure he knows this.

"The bravest thing I have ever done was continue to live when I wanted to die." ~Juliette Lewis

Endless Shadows: The Relentless Cycle of Depression

For years, this relentless cycle played out in my life. At first, I would reclaim a semblance of normalcy, feeling almost human again. But soon, an unsettling sensation would creep in, making everything feel off. My world became a haze of numbness and withdrawal. My faltering memory turned work into an uphill battle, a constant struggle to mask my cognitive lapses from my boss and coworkers.

Journal Entry (2013): I feel like there is something so terribly wrong with me. I wish I could die. I just want to die so bad. I just can't be happy. I can't even have peace in my mind. I think about such horrible things that I want to do to myself. I don't think I can ever change.

Then the darkness would descend. Depression would grip me fiercely, dragging me into a bleak abyss. I would be doing great at home for months, thinking that I was finally cured. I would work, stay active, and then I would start to withdraw. Usually, the first sign would be when I crept into my bed to hide immediately when I got home from work. During those times I would just bury myself in dark slumber and sleep the hours of my life away. I felt an unbearable sadness, emotionally distant and devoid of energy. Words escaped me; I would curl up in the fetal position, silently wishing for the end.

"Depression is like a heavy blanket. It covers all of me and it's hard to get up, but there's comfort in it too. I know who I am when I am under it." ~Shaun David Hutchinson

Paul watched helplessly as each day blurred into the next, until, inevitably, I found myself back in the hospital. This cycle of hospitalization became an unbreakable routine in my life. Doctors would adjust my medications, and I would sit through therapeutic group sessions, but nothing could pierce the veil of my depression. It was as if I was trapped in a shadowy underworld, desperately searching for a way out but finding only dead ends.

Journal Entry (2013, in the hospital): "I hate depression. I hate how it makes me feel empty and loathsome inside. I start to hate myself for who I have become. The depression has totally changed who I am. I feel so helpless and hopeless."

The possibility of ECT treatments arose again, and we faced the decision of whether to undergo another round. Although we knew what to expect this time, my obsession with wanting to die persisted, leaving us with little choice but to try the treatments again. Each treatment brought with it more headaches, sleepiness, and confusion. The headaches only worsened, as did my memory. I took several more weeks of medical leave to start the shock therapy, which meant several more weeks of my father driving in from out of state to take me to the sessions.

My father's support and unwavering commitment to my wellness never ceased. One particularly miserable night during visiting hours at the hospital, the weight of my situation felt unbearable. Family visits were limited to one hour, twice during the work week, and once on Sundays. That evening was especially poignant because I was supposed to be at the Marine Corps Ball with my dad. It was our cherished tradition. He loved to show off his young "date," and we would dance the entire night.

Dad and I were always each other's dance partners. At every family wedding, you could bet on us being the first to hit the dance floor and "cut a rug." Instead of twirling under the ballroom lights, I was confined to my sterile room, my heart aching for the joy I was missing.

I was distraught, thinking about how I was missing this special occasion with my dad. I sat in the dayroom during visiting hours, watching other families with a heavy heart. Then, I looked up and saw my dearest father standing in the doorway, dressed in his blue Marine Corps uniform, complete with a white hat and gloves. Overwhelmed, I could only cry as he held me in his arms, tears streaming down my face. We have always been incredibly close, and I know it was awfully hard for my parents every time I had to return to the hospital. Just imagine this precious memory: my dad, in his Dress Blues (which were anything but comfortable), driving two hours just to visit me for an hour, letting me know that he wasn't going to the Ball without me, his dance partner. That moment is etched in my memory.

Desperately, we would return to the next step in the endless cycle, which would be ECT treatments.

When I completed the series of treatments and went to follow-up appointments with the psychiatrist, I would always mention that my memory was worse every time. I was looking for guidance, remedies, or suggestions, but the only response I received was that it will pass and that I need to give it time. It was hopeless, and everything was spiraling. I can't count how many times I went into that office and complained about my memory, long and short, not improving, and the other problems I was experiencing. I developed problems comprehending what people were saying to me, problems multi-tasking, and problems making dinner since there were so many steps involved in making even the simplest of meals.

I confided in him about my disorienting experiences, telling him how I sometimes found myself lost without a clue of my surroundings, even in places I'd visited dozens of times. It was as if a fog suddenly descended, erasing my familiarity with the world around me. Yet, despite my plea for help, he offered neither answers nor suggestions to make my life more manageable. For weeks, I was mired in a deep, unshakable sadness, slowly realizing my problems were far more overwhelming than I had ever acknowledged. My days had blurred into a haze of lethargy, where staying in bed felt like the only option. I would rise just minutes before my husband returned, hiding my stagnation behind a facade of normalcy.

Negative thoughts ran relentlessly in my mind, an unending torrent that left no space for respite or hope. How was I supposed to conquer this never-ending darkness? Was it even possible to defeat something so insidious? Depression is a thief of joy, a harbinger of isolation, sorrow, and despair. I yearned desperately to break free from its grip, but after years of struggling, it felt as though I had exhausted every possible remedy. The following quote captures the conflicting emotions and challenges that come with living with both anxiety and depression, describing the inner turmoil of wanting and fearing, caring and feeling numb, all at once.

"Having anxiety and depression is like being scared and tired. It's the fear of failure but no urge to be productive. It's wanting friends but hating to socialize. It's wanting to be alone but not wanting to be lonely. It's caring about everything, then caring about nothing. It's feeling everything at once, then feeling paralyzingly numb." ~Unknown

Breaking the Silence: Advocating for Mental Health and Brain Injury Awareness

*G*rowing up, I was always very private, keeping my feelings and thoughts tightly sealed. In our household, an unwritten rule dictated that we never aired our dirty laundry outside the family. Yet here I am, sharing my story with the entire world! My aim in revealing these experiences is to provide you with an unfiltered view of how my struggles came to be. Just as one can't tackle Algebra without understanding basic math concepts, one can't comprehend my journey without seeing the full picture.

This book is not intended to shame the family who supported me through my battles with obsessive-compulsive disorder, anorexia, anxiety disorder, depression, and the neurological issues caused by ECT. My purpose in writing this book is to educate the world about mental illness, who it affects, and how society perceives it. Mental illness is often treated differently than physical ailments like cancer. When someone is diagnosed with cancer, families and friends rally together, offering support, meals, prayers, and anything else that might be needed. Mental illness, however, often lacks this same communal response, leaving those affected to navigate their challenges in isolation. Through my story, I hope to change that perspective and foster greater understanding and compassion.

> *"I wish people could understand that the brain is the most*
> *important organ of our body. Just because you can't see*
> *mental illness like you could see a broken bone,*
> *doesn't mean it's not as detrimental or devastating*
> *to a family or an individual." ~Demi Lovato*

When someone suffers horribly from depression, their mind often twists reality, convincing them that their loved ones would be better off without them. In those darkest moments, it's not a time for broadcasting their pain to the world. Unlike the joyous news of a new baby, which spreads through the family like wildfire, the somber announcement of someone being admitted to the hospital for mental health reasons is shrouded in secrecy. There's an unspoken agreement to keep it quiet to avoid unsettling everyone with the news. "Let's just keep this within the immediate family," they say. You won't find a Facebook post announcing, "Lisa is back in the psych hospital. She wants to kill herself again." That's the harsh reality of it.

I want to take a moment to express my heartfelt gratitude for the incredible friends and family who have stood by us time and time again, offering unwavering support in every possible way. When it comes to confiding in loved ones about delicate matters, it is often done in hushed tones, carefully avoiding words like "suicide" or "kill themselves." These terms are seldom spoken aloud, even by professionals, who typically ask, "Are you safe?" instead. The fear of workplace gossip looms large. No one wants their colleagues to discover they've been in a psychiatric ward. The potential for stigma and the intrusive glances of coworkers is a daunting prospect. Concerns arise about job security and the implications of taking medical leave, which inevitably reveals one's hospital stay.

One might wonder why anyone with a strong support network would consider ending their life. It seems incomprehensible; they appear to have it all – a stable home, the ability to pay bills, a respectable job. However, this is where the complexity and stigma surrounding mental illness are distorted. People often make assumptions, projecting their uninformed opinions onto someone else's situation without truly understanding it. They pass judgment without ever walking in that person's shoes. Mental illness doesn't signify a lack of external stability but reflects an internal battle where life becomes overwhelmingly burdensome, despite outward appearances. For some, this internal struggle becomes so intense that they see no other option but to give up.

From experience, I can honestly tell you that depression and mental illness are much more complex than one person struggling to cope with life. Mental illness encompasses the unique ways our brains function differently. Just as some people battle cancer or children are born with cerebral palsy, like my best friend Lisa, each of us carries a cross to bear. My mother, who grew up in a small Italian town and emigrated to America at 15, often recounts the saying from her hometown, "Each house has its cross." Someone's liver might fail, requiring surgery. Similarly, with mental illness, the brain itself is ill, not functioning as it should. There are countless illnesses that can affect the brain: Parkinson's disease, ALS, dementia, Alzheimer's, brain injuries from multiple concussions, developmental disabilities, and many more.

Mental illness is part of this spectrum. Yet, it remains shrouded in silence. Why don't we talk about our cousin with schizophrenia? It is likely because we've heard misleading information and formed assumptions based on it. Instead of seeking accurate knowledge, we often push the subject aside. In recent years, community education about various illnesses has improved significantly. October is Breast Cancer Awareness Month, March is National Colorectal Cancer Month, and May is Mental Health Awareness Month. The National Alliance on Mental Illness (NAMI) is a prominent organization dedicated to mental health issues. They offer support groups, advocate for legislation, and provide a voice for the mental health community.

A year ago, I reached out to the local chapter of NAMI, inquiring about support groups for people who have undergone ECT. The response was disheartening. Even the national office in Washington, D.C., confirmed the lack of resources and information. It struck me as ironic and troubling that in the very town where a hospital administers ECT, there was no support or relief offered by NAMI, also situated in the same town. Depression, a severe mental illness, often leads to ECT for those with the most critical cases. How could the leading mental health advocacy agency in the nation neglect the people who need the most help?

The disconnect between the need for support and the available resources underscores the broader issue of how society manages mental illness. It's a stark reminder that despite progress, there is still much work to be done in breaking down stigmas and ensuring comprehensive support for all aspects of mental health. They did offer me an opportunity to write a blog on it for them or to start a support group, but that leads me to believe that they have no knowledge about ECT. People who receive ECT usually end up with some type of brain damage, leading to problems with thinking, reasoning, organizing, and memory. If they were educated about it, they would know that it would be extremely difficult for someone after receiving ECT to even organize a group, let alone have the ability to maintain the process or write a blog about it. Writing a blog would be challenging, but drafting an entire book has been an immense struggle. I often repeated the same stories in different sections, forgetting they were already there. Even relearning how to use a computer was a daunting task. I've had tremendous help from others in writing this book. Basic tasks, like remembering household chores, elude me. I am utterly disorganized and struggle to meet deadlines.

Post-ECT patients need extra time because even the simplest tasks require enormous amounts of energy.

I've discovered that brain injury sufferers experience a unique fatigue. Physical and cognitive activities, such as doctor appointments, therapy sessions, or social functions, severely deplete our mental resources. Recently, I've been learning to break tasks into smaller steps, pausing to rest after each one. This is especially challenging for me. When I'm in the groove, like cleaning my closet, I fear that if I stop, I won't resume. My brain must be retrained to anticipate how activities will affect me and to plan accordingly. Just planning takes a lot of mental energy. Most "healthy" people don't need to plan ahead to avoid mental fatigue. However, anyone who has had multiple concussions, a car accident, a bad fall, or any other brain injury will tell you how exhausting it is to just attempt to live a "normal" life. The effort to stay alive is grueling.

Mind Over Matter: Daily Life with a Broken Brain

Journal Entry (February 2014): Today we talked about healing words and writing out our own "prescription." The things I must work on: 1. Learn to love life. Do more things outside; 2. Do daily affirmations; 3. Work on accepting myself; 4. Nurture my spirit. 5. Get better with self-care; 6. Sleep less.

After I went on disability leave and stopped working, things began to settle down. Although I still experienced the ups and downs of depression and struggled with sleep issues, I was no longer suicidal and didn't need hospitalization. Typically, my depression would stabilize, remain quiet for a while, and then gradually resurface. I continued to struggle with both short- and long-term memory issues. Even years after my last treatment, these memory problems persisted.

My psychiatrist's advice response was always to "give it time." But I was uncertain what this "time frame" meant. Would it be months or years? Indefinitely? Given how long ago the treatments occurred, one would think the problems would have been resolved by now. However, the treatments caused more than just memory issues; they had numerous cognitive side effects that influenced normal thinking, problem-solving, multitasking, decision-making, and much more.

Time, processing, and multi-tasking

I especially struggled with following directions. Whenever I stopped the car to ask for directions, I'd barely remember the first turn before everything else slipped from my mind. Cooking dinner felt like an insurmountable challenge, a chaotic juggling act with too many balls in the air. I'd fret over the meat, anxiously trying to avoid it being overdone or underdone, while simultaneously attempting to synchronize all the other dishes to be ready and hot. Cooking was never my passion; in fact, I loathed it. But the real issue was that Paul, after long, exhausting days at work, had to come home and tackle the task of preparing an entire meal. I know this has been a burden for him for many years, but I do admit that he has always been the better cook between us.

When we're tackling projects around the house, Paul patiently breaks down each task for me, but only one step at a time. Once I complete that step, we move on to the next. It's as if I need a personal assistant to guide me through every action. Writing this manuscript felt like navigating through the intricate maze in my mind. It demanded focus, memory, and computer skills, which I hadn't used in years. Organizing the narrative and figuring out the sequence of events has been daunting. Authoring a book is an immensely complex endeavor, presenting a formidable challenge for me. Remembering stories from my past is the hardest part. I've been leaning heavily on my journals and the support of my family to piece together the fragments. It's like there are countless jigsaw pieces in my mind, and every day is a struggle to fit them back together.

This has also had a great impact on my obsessive-compulsive disorder. I was always tidy and organized. Everything I owned had its appropriate place in the house. Since the treatments, I can't find anything. I put things everywhere and then spend days looking for them. I know a lot of people respond with, "Oh my goodness, I do the same thing!" It's definitely not the same, as I never used to do this. I spend days looking for my wallet and my glasses. After a month of searching for my glasses, I finally found them. My wallet has gone missing on multiple occasions. I cannot even count how many times I have lost my wallet. This is frustrating as it impacts another factor related to my mental health. I lose things that are important in my day-to-day life.

Another aspect I struggle with is managing money and numbers. During Christmas, if I'm buying something big or getting groceries and paying with cash, I get confused. While counting the money, I lose track of where I left off and have to start over again. A couple of years ago, during the Covid-19 pandemic, my running friends and I formed an informal group we whimsically christened The Pandemic Express. We envisioned having shirts made with a logo and everything, but with everyone busy and working full-time, the responsibility fell on me.

Despite my reservations about being the right person for the job, I went ahead. I contacted a local businessperson who specialized in custom shirts, duffel bags, and anything that could sport a logo. Once I finally determined the cost, I relayed the information to everyone in the group and began collecting the money. I knew I had to put it in a "safe place" where I wouldn't lose track of it, but despite my best efforts, I managed to lose and then find it again... four times. I warned them that entrusting me with cash was risky, but they didn't believe me!

My sense of time has also been disrupted. Ask me what month someone got married in 2015, and I'll draw a complete blank. Who was born first? What year did my son stop playing soccer? When did I coach soccer? Our family has visited numerous parks, and I'll often comment on how nice one is, only for Paul to remind me, "Don't you remember? You used to coach soccer games here." I have no recollection. How old was my son when he started to walk? What year did he dress as Mickey Mouse for Halloween? When did Uncle Bob pass away? When did we go to Italy? When was my first half marathon? When did we buy our house? The list goes on and on.

My concept of time has changed in other ways too. It's as if yesterday never existed and tomorrow is an unfathomable mystery, leaving me anchored solely in the present. Where are we going for Christmas? I have no idea; that's two weeks away. What am I doing tomorrow? I can't think about tomorrow until today is over. To cope, I rely on various memory aids: two whiteboards, constant reminders on my phone, and an abundance of sticky notes. If I ever stopped using sticky notes, I think the company would go out of business!

Journal Entry (June 2016): Today is Monday. I'm feeling very distant from myself and others. My brain isn't working quite right. I feel like I am clueless about everything. I can't complete sentences. I can't complete my thoughts. I'm starting to wish I were dead again. I don't want to think that way, but I feel useless. I used to be a social worker who could help people with their problems. Now I can't even help myself with my own problems. I want to be useful in this world, but my brain won't let me. I'm stuck and there is no way out. I don't feel happy. I feel useless. I can't figure out how to solve any problems.

In my search for answers, I discovered support groups on social media filled with others who have undergone ECT. I realized I wasn't alone in facing its consequences. With their permission, I've included some of their reflections on the aftermath of ECT. A clear, recurrent, and troubling theme emerged in terms of cognitive impairment and memory loss:

Q "ECT erased me. I couldn't see, I couldn't talk, I was in a fog for years with no personality, no emotions, just a lifeless body. It's like it took away the things that made me who I was. I will never be that person again."

Q "I have so much difficulty retaining any information."

Q "I don't feel close to anyone anymore because I can't remember our shared experiences."

Q "It's been ten years since I had my ECT, but my short-term memory loss is as bad as ever."

Q "I lost my entire lifetime of memories. I was forced to retire early. It has been a confusing, frustrating, and extremely difficult process."

Q "I don't know how to hang on anymore. I'm exhausted. So many regrets. Cognitively impaired for the rest of my life."

Q "I've known for a long time that it's not an actual treatment. If epilepsy causes brain damage, accidental electrocution causes brain damage, and especially lightning strikes cause brain damage, then why wouldn't ECT cause brain damage?"

Q "While dealing with really bad postpartum depression, I had 70 or more ECT treatments over a three-year period. I lost almost 90 percent of my memory and now have multiple problems with organization, retrieval, and processing information."

Q "Evidently, I have the same medical issues that electricians and anyone who works with electrical injuries have."

Like me, others also experienced severe forms of physical and mental exhaustion:

- "Exhaustion is brutal. I can manage a few days of work, but then I feel so tired that I have to sleep for a few days. It's not only physical but mental exhaustion too."
- "Everything that I do, whether physical or mental, is a struggle."
- "I didn't think or know that even five years later, the effects could still be happening."
- "I can no longer think straight, process, or remember what tasks to do."

Brain Noise

One hospitalization stands out vividly in my memory, largely because of the connection I made with a fellow patient. She was just a bit younger than me, with a sharp wit and a shared history of psychiatric challenges. We were both repeat ECT patients, and talking to her was a lifeline. She understood the frustration of memory lapses and the constant uncertainty of whether a task had been completed or not. What I remember most about her was our conversation about "The Noise." Somewhere along the line of ECT treatments, this dreadful buzzing sound had begun to echo in my head, a relentless presence that wasn't just the ringing in the ears that some people experience. It was a persistent crackling, a white noise that never ceased. I called it "brain noise." She knew exactly what I meant. Her empathy and shared experience were a beacon in a time of disorientation, grounding me in the understanding that I wasn't alone in this struggle.

Journal Entry (June 2018): Everything is so overwhelming. So much noise and so loud. All these people seem so happy, yet they are in a psychiatric hospital, and here I am stuck in my own head. I can't get it out of my head. It's just so scattered from one thing to another, and I can't focus. I just ran five miles last week, yet all I can do now is walk down the hall in my sneakers that don't have shoelaces. Why is this happening to me? It is so loud here. I can't concentrate on anything. I want peace in my mind, yet I can't get it. God help me through this. I am on my last nerve. Please God forgive me for being like this.

This persistent "brain noise" is part of my life now. I wake up with it, and I go to bed with it. There are times during the day that I have done too much, and my head actually starts to hurt. The noise in my brain becomes louder and more intense. It may sound strange, but I must take frequent breaks throughout the day between tasks to avoid headaches. It feels as if I've overtaxed my brain's capacity to function. If I type for an hour, go to my therapist, and then come home to try to clean something, it's as if my brain shuts off because it's too tired! The noise gets louder and louder, to the point that I have to lie down in bed and rest.

A year ago, my sister-in-law heard about my problems with the loud noise, so as thoughtful as she is, she bought me noise-canceling headphones. They do not get rid of the brain noise, but it does block out all the other noises, and then I can put some relaxing mood music on, and I am able to rest. I've become incredibly sensitive to noise, really any type of noise. Paul can be watching TV, and, every night, I ask him to lower the volume. He obliges, but I know his hearing is getting worse too! It's a bit of a conundrum: one person who can't stand noise and another who can't hear!

Communication

Last year, for my 50th birthday, my parents surprised my sister and me with tickets to Disney World. To say I was anxious would be an understatement! As mentioned, noise bothers me, and I don't handle crowds well. I decided to bring headphones on the trip, anticipating the cacophony of the airplane. I hadn't been on a plane since before my ECT treatments, so I had no idea how I'd react to being confined in such a noisy environment.

It had been a long time since my sister and I had spent quality time together. With all our children grown, it was the perfect moment to reconnect and rediscover our bond. Her presence was like a soothing balm, and she always had a wonderful way about her. Being a registered nurse was her dream, and she made it a reality. Her high spirits, positivity, and unwavering optimism were always a source of inspiration.

I was eagerly anticipating a vacation at Disney with my sister, though I was terrified by the sheer number of people we would encounter. The noise was overwhelming, and I still had a tendency to get disoriented and lost. I pleaded with my sister not to lose me, and my parents made sure she understood the gravity of this request. They half-jokingly warned her to keep me safe between the Jungle Cruise and Cinderella's Castle. It didn't take long for Terry to realize that managing me at Disney might be quite the undertaking. She had meticulously planned to hit three specific rides as soon as we arrived, but I was constantly lagging behind, getting swept up in the crowd. Without a leash to keep me tethered, she made me hold onto her shirt as we navigated the park.

Surprisingly, it worked well, and knowing I wouldn't get lost made it easier to relax and enjoy our time together.

As a sidebar, ever since my ECT treatments, I've struggled to find the right words to describe things. It has become sort of a game, albeit a frustrating one. On the plane, I wanted to ask my sister something and ended up saying, "Do you think the driver of the plane..." She corrected me with a smile, "Pilot, Lisa. He's called a pilot." Another time, while getting ice cream (it was my vacation, after all), I pointed and said, "I want those brown things over there!" My sister, ever patient, said, "Sprinkles, Lisa. They're called sprinkles."

Communication has always been the most awkward part of my life since the treatments. Forgetting the names of things and losing my words and thoughts mid-sentence has become a frustrating occurrence. I often find myself saying, "Just drop it," when I lose my train of thought. Thankfully, my family and friends understand that this is just a part of who I am now and that it likely won't change anytime soon. These communication challenges began in 2003, after my first round of ECT treatments.

20 years later, I still struggle with finding the right words. It's become a bit like a game of charades, where I describe what I'm trying to say, and the other person guesses until they get it right. It's actually a little funny if

you think about it. I try to laugh about it because if I didn't, I would probably cry. In the social media ECT groups, I have also connected with people who experience communication and emotional challenges in terms of emotional detachment and apathy:

Q "I have been so apathetic because of ECT and wonder what I can do to get my emotions back."

Q "I'm bothered because I don't seem to have that personal, emotional connection to people anymore."

Q "I had 23 bilateral ECT treatments over 15 years ago. I still have a very hard time making connections and processing emotions or feeling them at all."

Q "I have lost myself and I know that I will not be helped. I cry when I have to fill out any kind of form, and I have to tell whoever reads it that I can't remember dates and that I no longer have a sense of time."

Q "The effects that I have gotten from ECT are too bad. It's hard to accept that I'm never going to be the same. Even my family says that I am so different than before."

Sleep

I have always had problems sleeping. My parents say that I used to sleepwalk as a child. In the later part of the evening, I would walk into the living room, walk around in a circle, and sit on the couch. Then, a few minutes later, I would just get up and go back to bed. Throughout college, I was known for walking the halls in the middle of the night. I would get so restless and anxious that I had to get up and move. I would usually see the same people up. Some were studying, and some were just hanging out and relaxing. Nighttime was never good for me. After college and well into my adult life, the doctors diagnosed me with narcolepsy. It's a condition where something in the brain causes excessive daytime sleepiness. As a result, I frequently needed naps during the day, often in less-than-ideal places. At one of my jobs, I had my own office. Whenever the overwhelming urge to sleep hit, I would lock the door, pull down the shades, and curl up under my desk. The need for sleep was so intense that I had to close my eyes before my brain would simply shut down.

My sleep problems persisted after the ECT treatments, but now I was having night terrors as well. I would go to sleep and have extremely vivid dreams. I would see a dark figure coming into the bedroom. I knew in my terror that this man was going to rape and murder me, but I couldn't wake myself from this nightmare. He would get closer and closer until he was standing right above me. I would start screaming and yelling. Eventually Paul would need to wake me because by then I was flailing around, kicking, and screaming terribly. It was as if I could see the figure right there. Somehow, I was asleep but partially awake. I would try to scream, but sometimes my mouth would open and nothing would come out. I would feel paralyzed and unable to move my body.

This has continued for years, and I was completely exhausted during the day. I had to take frequent naps because I was so tired and also because I was afraid to go to sleep during the night because I feared that it would happen again. I have had people say to me, "Oh yeah, I've had them too, they're awful." I will tell you that these people have no idea how traumatic it is to have night terrors. Every night it was the same thing, and every night I would wake up kicking and screaming, not knowing how to wake myself. I would wake up with post-traumatic stress disorder. I felt violated and robbed of one of my essential needs.

What was strange about these dreams was the sense of paralysis that gripped me whenever I tried to escape the man pursuing me. I often thrashed around so violently that I would fall out of bed, waking up with bruises on my head, hips, and legs. Despite my efforts, I couldn't prevent it. Eventually, a family member suggested getting a side rail, like the ones used for kids transitioning to a big bed. We got a half-side rail and attached it to the bed, which at least stopped me from falling out, but it didn't halt the night terrors.

One morning, after Paul had left for work, I woke up stabbing the mattress. Thankfully, without a knife in my hand and no one to stab. Paul, a very heavy sleeper, rarely woke up to my nocturnal struggles. I felt like I was screaming so loud, but I didn't even know if any sound was coming out. Over the years, Paul has taken more than his fair share of beatings during my night terrors. I can't say for certain whether it's the shock treatments or the heavy load of psychiatric medications that causes my torment. Regardless of the source, I am haunted every night. Exhausted from sleepless nights, I yearn for rest but am paralyzed by fear at the thought of going to bed. It's just another chapter in the saga of bizarre psychiatric experiences that have unfolded in my life. I never asked for or deserved any of this.

I never expected that life would turn out this way. I never wished for the dark thoughts that plague me, nor for the relentless torment that feels as if it will never end. I never wanted to be traumatized every night as I tried to sleep. I have always strived to be a good person, dedicated to helping others through my work. How could someone with such good intentions suffer and carry such a heavy, relentless burden?

"No one wishes to have dark days, sleepless nights, grumpy mornings and this endless dark tunnel with no sign that it ever ends. Depression is not a choice." ~Robin Williams

Through every fracture, healing finds its way, stitching together *resilience* and *strength*, creating a masterpiece of newfound *hope*.

Silent Footsteps: The Lost Joy of Running

The fact that I was getting lost distressed me and my family tremendously. I remember one instance vividly: I went for a run while visiting my parents for a few days and got lost. I had recently taken up running again to keep me healthy and improve my mental health. I followed the same route every time I visited. It was a straightforward route with few turns, not overly complicated. I loved this path because it passed by a couple of schools where I could watch children playing. The route also crossed a bridge where a tributary flowed into the river, a picturesque spot that brought me peace. With its perfect balance of hills and level ground, the course was ideal for me.

However, my problem was that I would get so immersed in the rhythm of running that I lost track of my surroundings. Some doctors call this dissociation. I know many people suffering from the side effects of ECT who experience the same issue. My issue is that I do not remember that I might get lost when I go out for the first run in an environment. I forget how important it is to pay attention to where I am and where I am going. I always have my cellphone with me when I run in case of an emergency.

This time, I suddenly stopped. I anxiously looked around. Nothing looked familiar. I had run this route so many times, yet now I didn't recognize anything at all. I started crying, and I frantically tried to open Google Maps on my cellphone. My hands were trembling so terribly that I couldn't focus on searching on the app. I was starting to panic. I tried so hard to get Google Maps up, but I was so anxious and panicky that I couldn't think clearly enough to do it. I did know how to call my father because he was one of my emergency contacts.

I managed to call my dad, my voice trembling with uncontrollable sobs. As I cried, my breath grew ragged and shallow, each gasp feeling like a struggle. Sensing my distress, Dad gently guided me, asking questions about my surroundings to help me stay focused. He knew this route intimately, having run and cycled it regularly. Clinging to the phone, I spoke with Mom while waiting anxiously for Dad to find me.

A gold Toyota Prius eventually pulled up and stopped in front of me. Seeing my dad behind the wheel, a wave of relief washed over me. I collapsed into his arms, holding onto him tightly. In his embrace, I felt an overwhelming sense of safety and comfort. Dad had always been my rock, promising to protect me no matter what. Yet, even as I found solace in his words, a gnawing fear persisted. This episode was neither the first nor the last, and the weight of my depression grew heavier in that realization. Battling one mental illness was hard enough; the prospect of additional cognitive challenges made life feel unbearable. I felt hopeless. Something that I found joy in was now also ruined.

This was the first of several times when I would be out running and "dissociate." I found some kind of solution. I downloaded a tracker app on my phone, which would send a message to three family members, informing them of my location during the run and displaying it on a map. It would send another message when I completed the run. This was the best idea for them to keep track of me. The only problem with that tracker app was that it would drain my cellphone's battery. Then I would be totally lost and untraceable.

Soon after my terrifying running experience, I had another harrowing experience while out running. I was invited to go on a weekend retreat in Pennsylvania's beautiful farmland country. I was relieved to see there were only 15-20 women on the retreat. I was concerned about my anxiety levels. I have a tendency to start feeling overwhelmed and overstimulated by the things around me. Everyone seemed so laid back and calm. It made me happy to have received an invitation. There were lots of activities to choose from, like painting wine glasses, cooking classes, and different self-esteem activities, and just general support from the group of women. I really felt comfortable with this group because everyone was telling their stories about family, work, and different adversities they had faced in their lives. By the end of the first day, I had even made a couple of nice friends.

Journal Entry (April 2018): "Still at the retreat. I came across a Bible verse that hit me like a ton of bricks! The verse was Psalm 23, The Lord is my Shepherd. Even though I walk through the valley of the shadow of death, I will fear no evil." I was at death's door. I desperately wanted to be dead, but God carried me through it. I survived with the help of the nurses, Paul, and my family. When I think about what I've been through, I simply can't believe I am still alive."

Despite all the activities, there was plenty of time to relax. I seized the opportunity to go for a run and take in the beautiful countryside. I loved being outside, inhaling the fresh air and savoring the familiar aroma of home-made fires. It was such a comforting scent. Initially faint, it grew stronger as I ran, revealing that more people had their fireplaces burning than not. I figured that three miles was a reasonable distance to start with. I did not want to ruin the weekend by running too much and then not be able to participate in the actual retreat. I didn't know the area well, but I told myself that if I had to turn, then just keep it to right turns so it would be easy to get back. All I had to do to return to the retreat was turn left up the big hill. Simple enough, right?

The countryside was breathtaking, adorned with red, yellow, and orange leaves gently falling to the ground. Crystal-clear lakes shimmered with a delicate layer of mist hovering above. I was on a retreat after all, and capturing these moments with my camera added to the healing experience, making my time there truly enjoyable. Long wooden fences lined the fields where magnificent black, brown, and white horses grazed peacefully. Suddenly, I realized how much time had passed since I started. Checking my watch, I thought that I'd better head back.

I remembered my right turn rule, so all I had to do was turn around and make the first left turn I came to. Well, it seemed like it took forever, and because of my memory issues, I had forgotten the name of the retreat and the location. I started to slow down, and after it felt like I had been walking forever, I started to panic. All of a sudden I saw this beautiful old, white church with a high white steeple. I took a picture of it and realized that I had seen it once before. I looked at the photos on my phone, and there it was! I turned to the left and continued walking despite the intense pain in my legs. My mouth began to feel as dry as cotton. I had already finished all the water I brought with me and was feeling extremely parched. If I had to walk much longer, I would have to find a house and ask to refill my water bottle.

There was no cell reception out in the country side, so I couldn't contact anyone. I carried on following the road. I just focused on every step, hoping it was in the right direction. I eventually spotted what I believed to be the building. I went inside quietly, but everyone noticed my return. They were visibly concerned about me. Everyone was asking if I was okay and what had happened. I really didn't know what happened, but when I looked at my watch, the distance meter displayed that I had run well over eight miles. No wonder my legs hurt and everyone

was so concerned. The retreat director was just about to send someone out in a car to look for me when I came through the door. I sighed a long sigh of relief and went to my room to have a good long cry and go to sleep. This incident added to my rising anxiety and despondence to run. Now getting lost was a regular occurrence when I did something that really gave me joy. Running was one of the few things that actually relieved the depression. Why was this also being taken away from me? I wasn't about to stop. I needed something that made me get up in the morning. It was now more critical than ever that I had to address this issue, but I just did not know how.

I found a solution. For my own safety, my family decided I shouldn't go running alone. So, I discovered a running group listed by the local running store. They offered a "Couch to 5K" program, a six-week course that gradually transitioned participants from walking to running, steadily increasing the distance. My session began in January, in the frigid depths of winter. I distinctly remember thinking, "What the hell am I doing? It's insanely cold out here!" Not only was it freezing, but we also ran two nights a week and on Saturday mornings. The darkness of the evenings required us to wear reflective gear and carry flashlights. Having paid the session fee, I was determined to get my money's worth. The other runners appeared as hesitant as I was, which reassured me I was in good company. We were all in the same boat. Running regularly with the group became the most consistent exercise I'd done in a long time.

Sometimes we don't need advice, we just need somebody to listen.

Healing Paws:
Teddy's Miraculous Arrival

I recall a moment I finally sat up in bed after lying there for an entire week. Paul had work, and James had school. I had nothing to do or look forward to during the day. I felt withdrawn, isolated, useless, and, to be quite honest, lonely as all hell. I had no job to go to. I always put my whole heart into my social work jobs. That was me. I was a social worker, but not anymore. I had a career, and now I had nothing. No purpose. When I first became disabled and could no longer work, mornings lost their purpose. The word "disabled" grated on my nerves every time I heard it associated with me. It began with the endless Social Security paperwork, each form coldly branding me a "disabled person." As if my daily struggle with hopelessness wasn't enough, they slapped on labels like "broken" and "disabled," stripping away any sense of capability.

There was no 8:00 a.m. team meeting to review problem cases. There weren't any 11:00 a.m appointments at a patient's house, and there wasn't even a piece of paperwork to be filled out. No one needed me or my skills. I lost my identity, and that made my heart ache for years. I was lost, yet again. Lost in my little corner of the world, hidden and forgotten without a place to go, a person to counsel, or a platform to use my skills. After I stopped working, I felt like nobody needed me. I no longer felt important or experienced the satisfaction of helping families through troubling circumstances. As a social worker, often called Miss Fix-It-All, I handled the most challenging cases.

Whether it was a family of eight with no food, a homeless man without a mailbox to receive his Social Security check, or a Down syndrome couple who had just given birth to a full-term stillborn baby. That was one of the most difficult cases I ever had, but I managed it. No one could have prepared me to enter that hospital room and see a full-term, lifeless baby in her mother's arms. That is one part of my job that I hope I never had to experience again. Despite the challenges, I missed my job, where I

was excellent at solving problems and addressing difficult situations.

At work, I was needed. At home, my family was perfectly capable of taking care of themselves. I had just been released from the hospital, where I shared a room with a suicidal roommate (we were all struggling with suicidal thoughts) who often spoke about her service dog. Her dog helped with her anxiety attacks, prevented her from self-harming, and woke her from night terrors. He was able to be with her "out in society." At that time, I didn't leave the house at all. Even being in a store caused me overwhelming anxiety.

That was when I started repeating to Paul, "I need a dog." I longed for a dog I could love and that would love me despite all my problems. Growing up, we always had a dog. Our first was Sheba, a long-haired, purebred German Shepherd. Sheba was my best friend in the whole world, and we were the same age. Our backyard was large, beautiful, and fenced in, giving Sheba all the freedom she could wish for. She loved running back and forth along the fence line with the neighbor's dog on the other side, often for hours. One of her favorite toys was my dad's old tennis shoe, which she adored playing tug-of-war with.

Journal Entry (November 2015): I was talking to my roommate, and she said that she has one of those service dogs. She said they can be trained to know if your lithium levels are too low. They can also help with anxiety attacks, which I desperately need help with. It would be nice for me to have something like that to give me love and support, especially during the day when I'm all alone. I can't call anyone. They are all at work. I can't bother them at work.

So I sat on the bed and repeated, "Paul, I need a dog." I had given him the task of finding the thing that could be the key to my survival. Paul delivered! Teddy appeared like an answered prayer. He was over a year old and had long black hair with a white cross on his chest. He had funny ears that would change position depending on whether he was pleased with you or not. Teddy is a mix of Border Collie and Labrador Retriever. I knew Labradors were intelligent, but I had no clue about Border Collies. Through my daily experiences with him, I concluded he is a lovable maniac. He is an incredibly lively dog, brimming with more energy than I could ever hope to manage. Despite his boundless enthusiasm, his intelligence is truly remarkable. I delved into a book about Border Collies, which painted a vivid picture of their ceaseless need for exercise. These herding dogs, bred to tirelessly roam the fields from dawn till dusk, skillfully guiding cattle and sheep, possessed extraordinary stamina and drive.

Teddy gave me a reason to leave the house. I wanted to explore with my new companion and visit different parks. We bonded almost immediately. During those dark days when I lay in bed, engulfed in depression, he never demanded to go out or to be fed. Whenever I ventured to the kitchen, he followed me, his loyalty unwavering. He was always right by my side. We were attached at the hip! I aspired to train him as a service dog, but it was extremely expensive. Even a Board & Train program ran several thousand dollars, and just one hour with a professional trainer was $125. Determined, I turned to several Facebook groups, discovering that with the right resources, such as books, YouTube, and the support of the community, I could actually train him myself. It was easy to train him. He picked up tasks quickly, eager to learn, and always stayed motivated by the promise of treats as his reward.

I loved taking Teddy out on walks to different parks. The more time we spent together, the more I noticed how quickly he learned new words and commands. One day, I realized that if I let him lead the way, he would always take the same route back to where we started, which was usually the car. This inspired me to teach him the word "car." Every time we got into the car, I'd say the word and give him a treat. Gradually, I started with shorter distances, giving him the command to find the car. With lots of repetition, Teddy consistently found our car, no matter how far away it was parked. He never missed!

I spent countless hours online, reading about service dogs and watching YouTube videos on service dog training. Though I couldn't afford professional training, thankfully regulations allow for service dogs to be trained by their owners. I bought books specific to training service dogs and watched many videos. I consulted with professional trainers whenever there was something I struggled with. Soon, Teddy became my companion for running errands. Before Teddy, my depression and anxiety had kept me isolated at home. The thought of going into stores overwhelmed me, so I totally avoided going out.

Our first big outing was to the Dollar General store. Teddy wore his "Service Dog in Training" vest, and we walked in together. I needed to find something on the shelves, so I told him to sit. To my amazement, he stayed in the sit position the whole time. After paying, we stepped outside, and I said, "Find it. Find the car." Teddy walked confidently through the parking lot and led me straight to the car! Later, I trained him to sit next to the car before getting his well-deserved "cookie." Finally, I had a safe way to leave the house! This routine was great for my depression. Teddy needed more training, so we frequented different parks and stores, and my anxiety gradually decreased.

Teddy has been a true blessing when we venture out in public. My anxiety skyrockets in crowded places, and going into a store, especially a large one like Walmart, feels almost impossible. We avoid Walmart as much as we can. The hustle and bustle, people rushing around, bumping into us, and staring as if we were aliens make it unbearable. A typical scenario unfolds like this: I would ask an employee where to find something (since we all know how they hide things in the corners of aisles). They give me directions, but due to my memory issues, I only reach the general vicinity of this elusive household item. Then, I have to ask another person for help, and this cycle continues until I finally locate the Holy Grail of commodities.

Then, the next step would be to successfully get everything checked out and paid for. This would turn out to be an exhausting mission! While I'm at the checkout, I juggle managing Teddy and unloading the cart onto the belt. Teddy, ever so well-behaved, lies down patiently until I signal him to move closer. With him at my feet, I now face the rapid-fire cashier and the dreaded credit card machine. The cashier's words blur together in a fast-forwarded rush, making it impossible to keep up. I ask her to slow down, but by this time in the process, my anxiety has already skyrocketed. My hands shake as I attempt to navigate the cryptic credit card machine. The impatient stares and murmurs from the line behind me only add to the pressure, making it harder to focus on the buttons. At last, the machine beeps, a sound that always feels like rejection, and a wave of relief washes over me. Finally, I can escape this chaotic ordeal. Then Teddy comforts me once again. "Teddy, find it! Find the car!"

I let the leash out so he could walk in front of me. He goes in the general direction of the car and methodically stops after each car to look up and see if it's our car. He does this until he leads me directly to the car, and then he sits down and looks up to me with those eyes as if to say, "Did I do OK, Mommy?" Well, I make such a fuss and tell him "Yes" and "Good boy!" "Good, find the car." I give him lots of treats and hugs, and he knows he has done his job perfectly!

What a relief it always is to escape busy, cluttered, and unfriendly public spaces like stores, returning to the comforting presence of just Teddy and me. We are a team, a partnership that holds immense value. Despite my "disability," I fit perfectly into our two-man squad.

Teddy is like my personal assistant, always by my side, helping me navigate every interaction. Even if I falter, his unwavering love and desire for my praise and attention remain constant. In many stressful situations, knowing he will rescue me has become my saving grace.

I began by walking with him, gradually transitioning to running. The runs were challenging at first, as he would eagerly pull ahead, causing us to trip over each other, sending me sprawling to the ground. We worked with a trainer who taught us to tune into each other's movements. Before long, he was trotting in a perfect heel, matching my pace with ease. We started running locally, which helped me get out of the house more. We went through a series of dog training classes, including getting his "Canine Good Citizen Certificate." Having Teddy was a godsend because I had problems with getting disoriented even in places that I frequently went to. Later, I found through a Facebook group for ECT survivors that getting disoriented was one of its side effects. Teddy had an amazing sense of direction. When we were driving to see my parents, he would recognize their exit off the highway and start whining.

Through all of our training runs, he knew exactly where to go. If I tried to make a different turn that was not part of our route, he would pull me in the other direction.

With the right combination of commands, I could teach him to find our car from anywhere. This helped immensely with my tendency to get disoriented. He began accompanying me everywhere, even to my running group. Initially, he was so overexcited and completely out of control. However, with the right training, he learned to calm down and run safely by my side. Before long, he was joining me in races, 5Ks, 10Ks, and even half marathons. He effortlessly kept pace.

He never seemed out of breath, trotting alongside me for countless miles. As of the time of writing this book, he has completed five half marathons and one full marathon. People often asked, "You're going to make your dog run 26 miles?" I would laugh and reply, "You should be more worried about me!" For him, running was pure joy, like playtime. His eyes would light up, and his ears would perk with excitement at the mere mention of a run. It was as if he were a little kid, always eager for the next adventure. It became increasingly upsetting when we were out and people would comment on him, saying, "Oh, what a beautiful dog. Are you training him for someone?" I'd respond with a simple, "No." Then came the truly frustrating part: "You mean he's your service dog?" "Yes," I'd reply. Too often I was then asked, "Are you blind?" "No." And with that, they'd just walk away.

Being disabled when you appear perfectly fine presents its own unique challenges. Yes, I could run three miles, and I could begrudgingly go to the store. I could speak and interact with people without issue, yet I was still disabled. The responses and looks I get from people are outrageous. Who are they to judge whether I am "disabled" enough to need a service dog? Conflict usually starts when I need to explain that I have a service dog because my brain isn't functioning well. He draws a lot of attention; people tend to notice him, and then the questions start. People love to see him in public and love to comment on how sweet, well-behaved, and gorgeous he is. As I am usually reserved and not used to getting this much attention, I wasn't prepared for all the attention we would get from perfect strangers. And they were all wondering why a seemingly normal and functional looking person would need a service dog.

You see, I have an "invisible disability." On the outside, I look perfectly fine. I even run marathons. So why should I, of all people, need a service dog? It's as if people believe that without visible symptoms, I don't deserve one. Countless times I've been asked, "What kind of service dog is he?" It feels as intrusive as asking a stranger about their medical history. These interactions reveal a deep misunderstanding about disabilities that isn't immediately apparent, leaving me to navigate not only my condition but also the constant judgment of others.

Traveling everywhere with Teddy has brought about many defensive interactions. One of the toughest has been dealing with discrimination. I've been denied service at restaurants and even at the local lake because they don't allow dogs. When I tried to explain that, under the Americans with Disabilities Act (ADA), service dogs are allowed wherever the public is, they demanded to see his papers. However, the ADA does not require any official certification for service dogs (though some websites do sell illegitimate ID cards).

Despite all these challenges, having Teddy has been incredibly therapeutic and life-changing. With him by my side, I began running more fearlessly and consistently with my running group. This routine, combined with Teddy's presence, significantly improved my depression and minimized some neurological side effects from the ECT. The more I ran, the less pronounced my neurological symptoms became. My thinking became clearer, I was less forgetful, and my judgment and thought processes improved. While not completely cured, I became functional enough to manage daily life. Remarkably, it's been five years since

I last needed hospitalization for depression and suicidal thoughts.

Five years without hospitalization is a significant milestone for me, and I attribute it entirely to consistent running. I believe the increased blood flow to my brain has positively impacted my brain injury. However, if I stop running for any length of time, my cognitive symptoms return. To remain functional, I have to keep running. I can't imagine what I would do if I couldn't run. I'd likely revert to the way things were before, with significantly poor memory, trouble processing conversations and reading, frequent word-finding issues and stuttering, difficulty completing complex tasks, and deep depression. Teddy has been crucial in helping me maintain this running routine. My life depends on it.

With Teddy in my life, I no longer felt so alone and isolated. I still had bouts of depression, but during those dark times when I lay in bed, Teddy would lie there with me for hours. He never asked for anything. He was so patient and caring, he never asked to go out or for food or water. Obviously, I cared for him and made sure his needs were also met despite my situation. He also gave me a reason to get up. We spent countless days just lying in that bed, and he never once barked or showed any signs of needing anything, not even to relieve himself.

Teddy has also been great at helping me with sleep problems and night terrors. When he senses a night terror is happening, he will lay his body right across my chest to wake me up. It's hard not to wake up when you have an 80-pound dog on your chest. Teddy became my confidant and companion. When I felt overwhelmed, I'd just lay in bed with him, rubbing his belly while he wagged his tail with excitement. He had a habit of walking by when I was sitting in a chair and purposely nudging his head under my hand, always ready for petting and affection. His lovable nature and constant need for attention brought a sense of warmth and comfort into my life. Teddy gave me a new purpose. With him by my side, the possibilities seemed endless, and I found the courage to face the world again. My loyal friend had become my anchor. Together, we faced each day with renewed hope and strength.

Pillars of Strength: Faith, Family, and Friends in Times of Turmoil

There is an aspect of my life that I haven't discussed yet: religion. As mentioned, I come from an Italian Catholic family. I was raised that way. I went to Sunday School every week, and I received all the sacraments. Many people fall out of religion when they are in their teens and after, until little kiddos come along and then they come back to church for the baby to be baptized. At least that is what I have been observing with the current generation. Religion has always been a cornerstone of my life, shaping many of my choices, including the decision to choose a life partner. Paul and I first crossed paths at a spiritual retreat, where our shared Catholic upbringing became a profound connection between us. Our bond went beyond mere affiliation; we both actively practiced our faith. While we cherish our Catholic traditions, we also celebrate the diversity of our friends, who come from a range of religious backgrounds. I've always harbored a deep curiosity about different religions and their unique practices, seeking to understand both the distinctions and the commonalities with my own faith.

I once worked with a Hispanic woman who was at 20 or 30 years my senior. She was Pentecostal, and I often found myself asking her about her church, whether they practiced communion, if they used an organ, and what kind of music they played. Her church was lively, vibrant, and energetic, filled with loud singing, raised arms, and powerful, distinct sermons. She enjoyed sharing her spiritual experiences with me, and I took great pleasure in learning about her faith. Some people tend to shy away from exploring different spiritual paths, believing that their own form of worship is the only "right" way. I don't share that mindset. I've met people from various parts of the world and have taken an interest in learning about their cultures and religions. When it comes to faith, I believe we all share the same God, though our ways of honoring and communicating with God differ. Despite these differences, it remains the same God. I choose to be Catholic and practice my Catholic faith, embracing the diversity of beliefs around me.

It is important that someone has faith in a God, or a spiritual entity, and attempts to face life alone without depending on a higher power. Depression and mental illness can significantly impact not only your spirituality but also your belief system. We have all felt hopeless. It is those hopeless moments that define us and our faith. For some people, their experiences of deep depression have distanced them from believing in a God. It is such a dark place to be when you are in the mire of depression. In my opinion, the moment someone becomes suicidal is when they have lost all hope. Hope is the crucial element that determines whether we choose to live or die. I have seen others endure prolonged battles with depression, yet they still manage to find a glimmer of light at the end of the tunnel. It doesn't matter where this light comes from; what matters is its presence. For some, that light may be God; for others, it may be their child or another loved one. It varies for everyone. Those who have not experienced severe depression cannot comprehend how dark things can get. When that light dims into darkness, it becomes a matter of life or death.

In every fiber of one's being, it becomes a matter of life and death. Cancer is about life and death. When people hear someone has cancer, they shockingly ask, "Oh my God, has it spread?" Of course, people always assume that if the cancer has spread, the person is likely to die. With depression, "it has spread" is synonymous with asking, "Have they lost hope?" That is the critical difference. Many people believe that overcoming depression is merely a matter of willpower, thinking that one must simply force themselves to get out of bed each morning.

However, if a person has lost all hope, there is no light in their world. Nothing remains to anchor them to life. Nothing can keep them alive, no God, no religion, no child, no family, nor anything else they treasure. Most of us are "repeat offenders." Experiencing a single bout of depression is one thing; having it dominate your life like a relentless cancer is another. Depression, much like cancer, is always present in one form or another, lurking in the background. Remission in cancer means no active disease and no signs of it in the body. Similarly, when someone emerges from depression and enters remission, it seems as if the depression has temporarily vanished. To those around us, it appears we're finally free from its grip, and life can return to normal. However, for survivors of both cancer and depression (or any mental illness), our internal reality is starkly different. We constantly wonder, "When is it coming back?" It's never a matter of if it will return, but when.

When depression resurfaces in those who have battled it before, it can feel like an inevitable return, causing us to lose hope. The thought of putting my family through this again is unbearable; I cannot endure it once more. Each reappearance serves as a stark reminder that we may never completely rid ourselves of this relentless condition. We may spend our entire lives grappling with severe depression or fearing its return, but in these moments, hope becomes crucial. I find profound insight in quotes from those who have eloquently captured the importance of hope. Desmond Tutu reminds us, "Hope is being able to see that there is light despite all the darkness." It is through hope that we find something to live for, something greater than our depression. Charles Haddon Spurgeon captures this sentiment perfectly: "Hope itself is like a star – not to be seen in the sunshine of prosperity, and only to be discovered in the night of adversity."

Even when life is uncomfortable and problems seem insurmountable, Michelle Obama's words offer reassurance: "You may not always have a comfortable life and you will not always be able to solve all the world's problems at once, but don't ever underestimate the importance you can have because history has shown us that courage can be contagious, and hope can take on a life of its own." And as Kristin Armstrong wisely notes, "When we focus on our gratitude, the tide of disappointment goes out and the tide of love rushes in." Hope, in all its forms, promises us a force strong enough to guide us through the darkest times and help us emerge on the other side, still alive.

In my world of depression, I have always had my faith in God. I was always reminded of this key Bible verse, and I held onto it:

"The Lord is my strength and my shield:
my heart trusts in Him, and he helps me."
~Psalm 28:7-8

Faith endured and was the one force that has been with me through this entire lifetime with depression. For those who do not believe in God, this is an unfathomable concept. For these people, when you die, there is nothing. Nothing. Nothing to redeem you. Nothing to help you believe that there is something more to this life. There is a song by Stephen Curtis Chapman that I love to listen to. The words go something like this: "But there's more to this life than living and dying, more than just trying to make it through the day. More to this life. More than these eyes alone can see. And there's more than this life alone can be." I didn't sit down to write today with the intention of writing down those lyrics. I haven't heard that song in years. But it is the truth and I was reminded of it. We all want to know that there is something more than getting through a bout of depression and then just waiting for that depression to come back so we can do it all over again. God has always held my heart and attention. I grew up knowing Him, experiencing spiritual connections through youth retreats during my teen years. In adulthood, my husband Paul and I met at a retreat, and God has been the bond that connects us. Even when everything else has failed, God has remained a constant presence. So, you might wonder, how could I reach a point of hopelessness and despair?

We are all human and experience the full spectrum of emotions in the vast ocean of life. Some people gaze into that sea and see dolphins, whales, and beautiful deep blue waves. But when I'm depressed, I look into that immense body of water and see a shark's dorsal fin, circling like Jaws, mimicking my pace and direction, relentlessly following me even as I try to escape to the shore. If my beach and ocean are destined always to have that one hungry shark, how can I ever close my eyes and find peace? For me, it is my faith that provides the peace of mind to close my eyes and rest before the next wave hits. I believe there's more to that one menacing shark in the ocean. I envision millions of dolphins swimming swiftly, leaping joyfully from the water, only to dive back in and repeat their merry ritual. I know there is a great blue whale out there, waiting for me to venture out on a boat and reach over the bow to touch its smooth, soft skin.

How does this vision translate to actual life with depression? If I practice diligently and hone my swimming skills, maybe I can navigate past the daunting great white shark to reach the magnificent blue whale. Hospitals strive to equip us with the necessary tools to combat depression, regardless of its timing or duration. When my depression hits hard, my immediate reaction is, "Oh my God, I can't go through this again. I can't put my family through this again." When I fall into that deep, dark place and I don't even hear the people around me talking, somewhere in all of that babble, God is always there encouraging me to swim. Trust my skills. Trust my many years of prayer, retreats, going to church for activities, and meeting spiritual people who will act like God would want them to and catch me when I fall. In running, my coach Joe always says, "The hay is in the barn. Trust your training." Similarly, with depression, it means that while I am not in the throes of it, I should practice the skills I will need when facing that metaphorical shark.

I strive to attend church during the week at 8:00 a.m. Weekends are challenging due to my anxiety, which makes it hard to cope with large crowds and loud noises. There's a dedicated group of older individuals who attend mass every weekday without fail, rain or shine. Their unwavering commitment amazes me. Praying at church brings me closer to God, and being surrounded by spiritual, genuinely good people strengthens my resolve. It reassures me that I am loved by God, reflected in the people around me. When I was in the emergency room, confined to a tiny lockdown unit with only a bed, huddled on the floor in the corner, it was the chaplain who came in, kneeled beside me, wrapped her arm around me, and softly sang and prayed with me. I can remember being in that room and being terrified. The other patients, unwilling to voluntarily consent to go to the psychiatric hospital, were loud and aggressive. A thick wall and small window separated them from the nurses. As the patients yelled, screamed, and became violent, I feared for my life. Huddling in the corner, I began to pray.

Yes, pray! Because when I am not depressed, I strengthen my weapons to get me past that shark. I pray harder and deeper that God will increase my faith. Not only in good times, but also in troubled times when I'm desperately trying to outswim that shark. In the good times, I focus not only on praying more fervently and deepening my faith but also on surrounding myself with genuine people of strong character. It's not about their religious affiliation. Some of my closest friends are from different religious denominations and include Methodists and Presbyterians and smaller Christian churches. I even have a close friend who doesn't attend church. I'm not implying she lacks belief in God; on the contrary, I think she does.

However, other aspects of her life hold greater importance to her. This doesn't diminish her in any way; she is, in fact, one of the strongest women I know. She has faced numerous challenges, metaphorically swimming past sharks since childhood. Her resilience is a testament to the support of her family and other compassionate individuals. Was God present in those family members? I like to believe He was and always will be. Religion is different than spirituality. Yes, I continue to actively practice being Catholic by going to church, saying my rosary (a gift from my grandparents), and helping others. We may be different religions, but there is only one GOD. We each choose to practice our faith in diverse ways.

While working towards attaining my Master's degree in Social Work, I had the privilege of working at a drug and alcohol treatment center. At Alcoholics Anonymous, the concept of having a sponsor is fundamental. When someone is newly sober, each day without using substances represents a significant achievement. Participants are encouraged to find a sponsor to guide them through their journey. A sponsor refers to someone who has personal experience with the program and recovery. These sponsors have walked the same path and are invaluable in helping others achieve and maintain sobriety. Sponsors may not hold advanced degrees in substance abuse and recovery; they are regular people who have lived through the challenges themselves.

The Alcoholics Anonymous program is known for its effectiveness across a diverse range of individuals in need of support. These sponsors help keep individuals grounded and focused, discussing a "Higher Power" that is meaningful to each person. In Alcoholics Anonymous, the term "Higher Power" refers to a guiding force through life's difficulties. By strengthening our faith in whatever we conceive that Higher Power to be, we equip ourselves with the resilience needed to combat depression and mental illness. When we are not actively struggling, we prepare ourselves to face these challenges when they resurface.

For me, that "Higher Power" is God Almighty. I don't impose my beliefs on others, but I strive to live simply, as Jesus did, focusing on being present and doing God's work. I feel that God is guiding me to write this book, to reach out to the many people who suffer in silence and need reassurance that mental illness, depression, and recovery are real and shared experiences. Those who have been through similar struggles are best equipped to walk alongside others, helping them navigate their journey from dark times to brighter days. Music has also always been a source of deep comfort for me, a refuge that began during my first retreat. There, we sang songs accompanied by guitars and melodies that spoke of strength, family, pain, love, and redemption.

Throughout college, I found solace in playing my guitar, and on tough days, I retreat into the embrace of music. When the pain in my head becomes overwhelming, I lie down with my ear buds in, letting soft, spiritual songs carry me away. These songs, filled with hope, are exactly what I need when I'm struggling physically, emotionally, or mentally. Recently, when the pressure in my head and the noise in my ears became unbearable, I turned to music once again. The first song that played was Steven Curtis Chapman's *Jesus Will Meet You There*, from his 2009 album "Beauty Will Rise" by Sparrow Records, a song that met me right where I needed it most.

Jesus Will Meet You There
When you think you've hit the bottom
And the bottom gives way
And you fall into a darkness
No words can explain
And you don't know how you make it out alive
Jesus will meet you there

When the doctor says, "I'm sorry
We don't know what else to do."
And you're looking at your family
Wondering how they'll make it through...
Whatever road this life takes you down
Jesus will meet you there

He knows the way to wherever you are
He knows the way to the depths of your heart
He knows the way 'cause he's already been
Where you're going
Jesus will meet you there...

Parallel to religion, I look to running and my running community for support and understanding. In running, we do different types of runs, so there is a variety of skills we need to guide us through those difficult runs, whether it be a 5K (3.1 miles), a 10K (6.2 miles), a half (13.1 miles), or a full marathon (26.2 miles). The road is not always flat; there are hills and bumps. The sidewalks are a nightmare, and sometimes we must run in the street to avoid the bad sidewalks. The roads are also not always clear and open or in a good condition. When I run with my group, we keep checking to make sure that everyone in the group is safe. We stop at traffic lights and intersections to make sure everyone gets through the intersection safely. Sometimes there is a coach in the front and one in the back. Sometimes there is only one coach who has to keep track of everyone.

The people I run with have different motivations. Some aim to complete their first 5K race, while others enjoy the camaraderie of the group. Running together often feels like a form of therapy. We share our problems as we run, and fellow runners offer advice or simply lend their support. My running group is well aware of my psychiatric and cognitive problems. They are aware that I run with Teddy to ensure I don't lose my way or venture into the wrong side of town. When I stutter while I am running, they know that it is a result of all the shock treatments that damaged my brain. They accept me as I am. When we talk about the surprise party I organized for Joe last year, which I don't even remember, they know it's just part of who I am now. I have never kept my problems a secret, and I didn't hide them from my friends and family. We've always been open and honest about my psychiatric hospitalizations, the shock treatments, and

the adverse side effects of the numerous medications I take.

You might think that knowing these things about me would scare people away, or make them avoid getting involved in my life, but that isn't the case at all. In fact, I've received more support than most. My close friends, family, and running community understand that when I'm not running, it's because I'm dealing with another migraine or the noise in my head is so loud it feels like it might explode. They understand that my hands and legs are shaking because my anxiety is taking over. They know Lisa is having a hard time and wonder how they can help her through it. I know I am luckier than most people. I have genuinely supportive and loving friends and family who would move mountains to help me through this bout of depression. They have seen me struggle through many days, and it also really upsets them. They have immense understanding and empathy, and I know that I don't have to struggle alone.

Strength in Unity and Lifelines: The Power of Family and Friends

The oppressive weight and darkness of deep depression and mental illness are burdensome and difficult to comprehend. Its unique form of torment slowly drains the vitality of those around you. I know that countless individuals endure profound suffering and feelings of isolation as the medical community often fails to acknowledge their experiences. For years after my treatments, I visited my psychiatrist, lamenting my impaired short- and long-term memory. Each time, I was advised to "give it time." My feelings and suffering were easily dismissed. This response made me feel as though my doctor believed I was imagining these symptoms, dismissing them as mere figments of my imagination. As

if what I was experiencing was in fact all in my head... (Did you catch that pun?)

When validation and genuine support are absent, a sense of despondency seeps in, causing us to question ourselves and feel inherently flawed and alone in our experiences. This lack of acknowledgment makes us believe something is fundamentally wrong with us, isolating us further. When our feelings and experiences are ignored and dismissed, deep depression begins to creep back into our lives. This cruel cycle intensifies with each occurrence and repetition. My friends and family are weary of my constant complaints about migraines and the relentless noise in my head that prevents me from leading a meaningful life. If I can't achieve anything significant, maybe I don't even belong here. Perhaps I shouldn't be alive. Who would miss me if I were gone? Certainly not my doctor who dismisses me and fails to acknowledge or validate anything I share.

When we reach this point of desperation and despair, it is vital to seek and feel that one emotion that differentiates life and death. This emotion is called HOPE. Losing hope makes us start to doubt our purpose and worth. I start to lose hope when I realize that my family could easily go on without me. However, the truth is: if I were to end my life, it would undoubtedly bring immense sorrow to the lives of my friends and family. There would be a sense of loss, a sense that things are different now that Lisa is gone. No, the world won't end, but people in my life would experience loss, regardless of its magnitude, however great or small.

I often underestimate my friends and family. I see everyone else busy living, working, being productive, and making a difference while I am at home, struggling with the disabilities and limitations caused by depression and the impact of various treatments on my cognitive abilities. This leaves me feeling disconnected, as if I no longer make any difference in "that" world. However, I realize that I do have a significant impact on their lives. Depression casts a shadow over relationships, causing them to suffer and function suboptimally. People become sad, doubtful, frustrated, and often lost. This is the stark reality for both patients and their families.

It is during these moments of intense doubt and overwhelming despair that we may feel the strongest urge to seek release from this earth. It's a cycle where self doubt increases and that urge to leave becomes even deeper. At that stage, our families are also not functioning at their best. They are battling to help us, yet simultaneously wrestling with feelings of hopelessness and a sense of being utterly powerless themselves. At these obscure times, we feel as if we are drowning in quicksand, and our families must be at their strongest to pull us out. They are fighting to help us, feeling hopeless and helpless. In these moments we and our families must be stronger than ever to pull out of this quicksand. For me, it is quicksand because I rapidly decompensate in these situations. My depression can escalate, reaching a severity where, within a day or two, I find myself back in the psych ward.

Like I said, mental illness is gruesome in its own way. This tragic story of depression is challenging for anyone to see play out in front of their eyes if it is related to a loved one and family member. They witness our gradual descent down that treacherous slope and hesitate to speak, fearing the impact their words may have on us. It's hard for them to watch us slowly going down that slippery slope and they don't want to say the wrong thing for fear that it will "put us over the edge."

They are so afraid of upsetting me, even now that I am in a healthier space. They choose their words carefully, aiming to offer support without inadvertently provoking feelings of anger, frustration, or sadness within me. Hoping that they can say the right thing to me and not say anything that will make me mad, angry, or sad. My mental illness fluctuates so drastically from moment to moment that just when you think you've got a grasp on it, it slips away and changes direction, leaving you constantly adjusting and adapting to its unpredictable shifts. I recall times when I was thriving. During those times, I practiced healthy nutrition, had an active and happy social life, and my thoughts were positive. Even in supposedly "healthy" times, things could suddenly change at the drop of a dime, and an episode would become inevitable. My family often tells me that I shouldn't worry because it's not such a big deal. The signs of depression are so clear that they can't be missed.

It is quite daunting because at those times, people can just look at me and visibly see that I am depressed. I isolate myself and withdraw completely. I stay in bed all day. Conversations are succinct and limited to "yes" and "no" answers. I do not bathe for days or brush my teeth, staying in the same set of clothes for days. I find myself in the fetal position, curled up in a little ball in my bed at those times. I would silently suffer and plead that God would have mercy and just relieve me of this pain and end my misery for myself and my family's sake.

My family watches these episodes, and they fear for my safety. They know that I am in shark-infested waters and that the predators are closing in on me, but they feel helpless because they can't swim and they

don't have the means to rescue me. My family is unsure of their actions and their words, fearful that their words might inadvertently steer me toward the jaws of that metaphorical great white shark. I can't imagine what it must be like for my husband to come home every day, not knowing in which state he will find me – dead or alive? Will I have overdosed? Will I have hung myself? What should he do when this happens? Mental illnesses such as depression are not perceived in such a way, but it is definitely a matter of life and death. Unfortunately, our families are along for the roller coaster ride. It's definitely not a joyful ride; it's frightening. Their roller coaster may not have loops, drops, and sharp, scary inclines in it like ours, but it's uncertain, steep, and treacherous.

How do we navigate supporting both them and ourselves while we're both riding our respective emotional roller coasters? The structure of the roller coasters remains the same. We know what it looks like and that we should get on it, but we are also scared of what is coming and of how fast, unstable, or intense the ride will be. Once you are on, there is no getting off. You must just ride it out, hoping you don't get sick or that the person next to you or behind you doesn't get sick on you. You may not know exactly where the big dips are, but you know they are going to be scary and deep because the car you are in is slowly creeping up the steep incline to the very high, unavoidable top, followed by the dreadful drop.

Ultimately, you have no control over the ride. Families of people with mental illnesses are on the same roller coaster. They are aware of the steep climbs and the scary dips, but they can't control it. They feel helpless on this ride. The steep part is coming, and they have no control over it. All they can do is hold on tight and pray that it will soon be over. When I am sick and deeply depressed, it's not just about what is happening with me and my brain. Much of it stems from the guilt I feel for causing pain to my loved ones. I know they are afraid to come into my room. I know that they doubt everything they say to me.

For years, my husband would ask me, "Are you safe?" Most of the time, the answer would be "yes." He would then ask me what he can do to help me. My response is always "nothing." But then he slips another question in, "What can you do to help yourself?" I always know when this question is coming, and I dread it because I really do not know. This happens often, and I still haven't been able to produce an adequate answer.

When I worked in hospitals and nursing homes as a social worker, we would always hear about the notion of "emergency preparedness." We heard it so much that our brains would go on autopilot whenever our supervisor would mention this. I never in a million years thought that I, myself, would use that term, but in the case of mental health, it makes perfect sense. Emergency preparedness means proactive practice of the precise actions required when a disaster strikes, ensuring readiness and swift response to mitigate its impact. It relates to coping ahead. Emergency preparedness is about practicing. The nurses immediately go to the emergency room, and start preparing beds for all the incoming patients. Usually, social workers offered desperately needed support not only to the patients but to the staff as well. We have worked this out ahead of time, so when the metaphorical bomb is detonated and ready to go off, and we know this is inevitable, we each have a specific job to do.

One person drives the "patient" to the hospital. They already know which hospital they will go to. Another person is assigned to make phone calls to specific people to let them know we are in trauma mode. Not only does the process flow easier, but individuals also feel a sense of contribution as they assist the patients in their unique and specific way. There is a profound desire to see that their assistance is meaningful, even if it is a small gesture or task. This provides a sense of fulfillment and purpose. Not only do things flow easier, but people feel like they are helping the patient in their own way.

Every person with a mental illness should prepare for the inevitable. We should all have a plan of things we should do when our moods and thoughts overwhelm us in the worst way possible. This action plan should include our family and friends, because we know for certain that we are not strong enough to do it on our own. Sometimes we repeat our actions, hoping that it will work this time around, but it doesn't. Sometimes the execution of our interventions requires creativity, and this would be the better course to follow.

Recently, I have been trying to think outside the box. Instead of the regular interventions, I came up with a few simple but effective ways to stabilize my mood. One thing I considered was watching a Robin Williams improv video. I know it sounds weird, but I also know that I cannot watch one of his videos without almost peeing in my pants from laughter! He was always gifted in being able to make everyone laugh and spread some joy. The reason he was able to do this is because he knew exactly what it was like to hate life and to hate having to get out of bed each dreaded day.

He knew how hard it is to get up, put on that fake smile, and pretend that we are happy. If you have never been depressed or in the middle of a mental health crisis, then you have no knowledge or experience of how

absolutely draining it is to the body and mind to have to pretend to everyone around us that we are happy and that everything is fine. Robin Williams suffered from severe depression, among other things, so he knew exactly what it was like to feel completely miserable and hopeless.

As we experience decline, our families witness it too, often feeling just as powerless, helpless, and hopeless as we do. Sometimes even more so. Yet, sometimes, a single person or event can pierce through that despair, revealing the promise of a brighter tomorrow beyond the horizon. During my last admission, I was particularly depressed, feeling disappointed in myself for having gone so long without visiting the hospital, only to find myself there... again. I cried and sobbed uncontrollably. One moment I was functioning normally, and the next moment I was praying for a car to hit me.

I was in my room, sitting on my bed, which was the one closest to the door. I looked up, and there stood my sister, Terry, tilting her head just enough for me to know that she felt sad seeing me this way. The fact that she was there and not my husband or parents (my usual visitors), completely surprised me. She entered my hospital room, approached my bed, sat down, and embraced me like never before. My older sister loved me enough to make that trip, not knowing what she would find when she got here. I knew that she was always busy as a nurse back home, and she was raising three daughters, so there was not a lot of time or energy (remember how mental illness sucks the energy out of them too) to make the long trip. She held me tight as if I were a newborn baby, holding my head to her chest while I cried. Finally, I was able to release all those emotions that were holding my soul hostage.

> "People cry, not because they're weak. It's because they have been strong for too long." ~Johnny Depp

Those feelings were toxic, and I knew it, but this hospitalization was different. After successfully avoiding hospitalization for so long, the reality of needing immediate admission suddenly hit me, leaving no doubt about the necessity of hospitalization.

Terry brought me a small gift bag, which I assume the nurses had already inspected and approved before delivering it to my room. Inside the bag was a magazine, a piece of chocolate, and a small, light blue leather-bound book titled *Jesus Calling* by Sarah Young. This devotional offers a brief reading for each day, designed to ground and steady the mind. Those of us with mental illness know how easily we can get trapped in our own thoughts. I find that when I read it regularly, despite the memory loss from ECT making it hard to remember, my thoughts become more peaceful, and I rely more on God for support when no one else is there.

Prayer for Depression

Lord, in Your goodness, help me to grow in faith and hope each day and trust in the future You have prepared for me. Lift me out of my depression, and hold me close to your healing grace. As we walk together during each moment of my recovery, teach me to place my worries and doubts in your hands. Replace the dark cloud of depression with true joy found in You alone. Thank You for my life, for the unseen blessings You've given me, and for being with me always.

Amen.

The Tools You Use
to Build Resilience

I have to be honest – there are no quick fixes in life. No magic bullets or instant cures. Beyond medication and therapy, I've had to equip myself with tools and strategies to manage depression and cognitive challenges. My message to you is simple: never give up and continue to seek what works for you. At times, encouraging quotes have illuminated my path, and reading these words has given me the strength and courage to never give up.

In my journey as a survivor of ECT treatments and depression, I have found solace and strength in the wisdom of those who have faced their own trials. Rikki Rogers reminds me: "strength doesn't come from what

you can do. It comes from overcoming the things you once thought you couldn't." Similarly, Theodore Roosevelt's insight resonates deeply: "Courage is not having the strength to go on; it is going on when you don't have the strength." When faced with disappointment, I draw inspiration from Joyce Meyer's perspective: "When it weighs on you like a rock, you can either let it press you down until you become discouraged, or you can use it as a stepping stone to better things."

Friedrich Nietzsche's statement "What does not kill you makes you stronger" reinforces my understanding that our experiences, both good and bad, shape who we are and contribute to our growth. The observation by Jimmy Lavine that "life is a balance of fear and overcoming it" is commonly associated with the concept of balancing fear and courage. Ultimately, Abraham Lincoln's words remind me that "In the end, it's not the years in your life that count. It's the life in your years." These quotes have become integral tools in my toolbox, helping me navigate the challenges of depression and reinforcing my resolve to live fully despite the obstacles.

Running has been my lifeline for navigating the turbulent shark-infested waters of depression. It triggers a positive chemical shift in my brain. Running with my group offers the psychological support of talking through my life challenges. When I joined this running group in 2018, I initially found it odd that we took a photo after every run. The next day, these pictures would appear on Facebook, accompanied by details of our distance and time. I didn't realize it at first, but those posts sparked a wave of encouragement. Comments like "Great job!" and "You killed it!" created a supportive cheering squad, providing positive affirmations that fueled my desire to run more and better.

Consistently running has significantly improved my mental clarity, particularly regarding the side effects from ECT, such as processing thoughts and understanding conversations. As my depression lessens, my productivity increases, which, in turn, boosts my self-esteem. I believe running is so effective because it enhances blood flow to the brain's deficient areas. I think more clearly and feel mentally healthier when I run three to four days a week. Running keeps me grounded. My mom is my greatest supporter. She can see the difference it has made in my life, and she frequently asks me, "Did you run today?" She knows that as long as I am running, my mental health stays in check. On days that I do not run, I have to reassure her that I am feeling fine and that I plan to run again tomorrow. Running is a form of therapy, and I cannot survive without it.

A couple of years ago, I suffered an ankle injury that sidelined me from running for seven weeks. With each passing day, I felt my hard-earned strength slipping away, and the isolation of not running began to drive me a bit crazy. The psychological toll was immense. My cognitive deficits and memory worsened, nearly reverting to the state they were in when I first left the hospital. This experience made me realize how essential running was to my well-being. When I finally rejoined my running group, I struggled to keep up and often had to walk because of the pain in my ankle.

One of my coaches, Susan, whom I deeply admired, understood the challenge of being forced to stop running due to physical illness. Despite battling cancer for years, she always had a smile on her face and continually encouraged us with tips and advice to improve our running. One day, as I stood on the sidewalk with tears streaming down my cheeks, Susan approached and gave me a heartfelt hug, despite her tiny stature. She related to me because she had been in the same situation many times. She encouraged me not to rush, advising that I should trust the process and keep moving, one step at a time. Pace didn't matter; it was about time on my feet. She was always there for me with a big smile and a comforting hug. I knew she had walked in my shoes, experiencing illness and the struggle to feel whole. She would become one of my biggest supporters when my dream finally came true (we'll get to that later!).

We all have something in our lives that has the ability to keep us grounded and healthy. Sometimes it's supportive family and friends, an Alcoholics Anonymous sponsor, writing in a journal, reading, or getting lost in music or artistic activities. The list goes on and on, and the possibilities are endless. The more grounding things we have access to, the more likely we are to survive the next bout of depression or mental health hurdle. For me, finding solace extends beyond simply running. It is supportive family and friends, friends at church who pray for me when I am having a tough time, phone calls from people in my life offering love and support, being consistent in taking my medications, and going to my therapist regularly.

These are essential tools in our toolkit that we must use to prepare for dark times. The more tools we have, such as family, friends, therapists, sponsors, yoga, exercise, good nutrition, and consistent medication use, the better equipped we are to navigate difficult episodes. While we may still face bouts of depression, having these tools in place ensures we have the necessary support to make the experience less intense and traumatic. I

don't think I truly understood the significant role a good therapist plays in helping to overcome hurdles until recently. If you are anything like me, you have probably had more than one therapist.

I cannot count the number of therapists I have had in my life. Some were very helpful, but they moved on to bigger and better things, leaving me to find a new therapist and navigate my chaotic life. It was not just about finding anyone, but someone who genuinely believed in me and my ability to work through problems. I have had therapists who spent the entire hour talking about depression and the importance of regular therapy sessions. The problem was, they were not actually doing therapy; they were just doing all the talking. They didn't teach me any useful skills and just rephrased the situation. Going to the wrong therapist actually made me feel worse; I was paying someone to help me, but I felt even more horrible leaving their office than I did when I first walked in.

A good therapist should be someone with whom you can have a fluent and meaningful conversation. Good therapists are experienced and qualified, but they should also have the wisdom to guide and coach you. They should ask insightful questions about different aspects of your life and challenge you to cultivate gratitude, practice positive affirmations, and improve your communication with family. They should teach you skills that improve your life. By recognizing the good things in our lives and appreciating their value, we shift our focus away from negative thoughts. Instead, we channel positive energy toward others and the things that matter most. Your therapist is supposed to guide you towards these types of thoughts.

I've found that shifting my focus to supporting others rather than dwelling on my own life has helped me avoid becoming consumed by my own troubles. This quote by Kristin Armstrong resonates with me: "When we focus on our gratitude, the tide of disappointment goes out and the tide of love rushes in." I have had many experiences volunteering in diverse ways. I've helped with food pantries, worked at missions with the homeless, volunteered in nursing homes as a friendly visitor, written Christmas cards to the troops overseas, and worked at the local soup kitchen. On one occasion, I organized a group of colleagues and friends to volunteer at a retreat house that was housing homeless men for two weeks. We prepared and served a full meal to these men, who were incredibly friendly and appreciative, grateful for even the smallest gestures. It was a life-altering experience for all of us involved, including my husband and my then eight-year-old son.

My son loved talking to the men, and they seemed to genuinely enjoy talking to him. He had no preconceived notions about homeless people and whether they deserved to be treated less respectfully than the rest of society. He was not critical, but just the opposite! He was one hundred percent respectful of those men, and for years he would often ask me, "When are we going back to the retreat house to feed the homeless?" It was an experience that shifted his focus from his own life and problems to offering help to others. I am now at a point in my life where I want to focus on helping others, shifting attention away from my own problems, such as the increasing cognitive challenges and the bouts of depression that might arise.

Maya Angelou says, "If you don't like something, change it. If you can't change it, change your attitude." In the same state of mind, James Baldwin agrees that "not everything that is faced can be changed, but nothing can be changed until it is faced." Recently, some of my cognitive side effects have worsened. While not earth-shattering, it is enough to make me realize that I need to draft this book now while I still have all my faculties. I have no idea where I will be in five years regarding my ability to think, solve problems, and communicate with others. This recent decline has ignited a fire within me, emphasizing the importance of sharing my story so that others can find comfort in their own recovery journeys. As I mentioned, many things can aid you on this recovery journey. None of them are easy, but they are all worth trying compared to remaining stuck or giving up.

FACT:

Running is one of the few activities that can grow new brain cells. Regular running increases the production of brain-derived neurotrophic factor (BDNF), which promotes neurogenesis in the hippocampus--an area crucial for memory and learning.

Training Against the Odds:
Let the Games Begin

In 2021, I was in excellent psychological and cognitive health. Early in the year, I completed a half marathon and felt like I was in the best shape of my life. I began to consider running a local marathon in October. Naturally, I had to think about how long it would take to finish, whether Teddy could handle 26.2 miles, and what it would be like with all the other runners around us. Whenever we ran in a group, I always stayed at the back to ensure no one tripped over him. I was well aware of the details and content of the ADA, so I knew the race coordinators had to allow Teddy to run with me. If they refused, it would be illegal, as it would be considered discrimination.

I had volunteered for the marathon before, so I still had the contact details of one of the race coordinators. I emailed him to explain that I wanted to enter but would be running with my service dog, giving him a heads-up. He said he would get back to me, which I thought was just a formality. However, a few days later, I received an upsetting response stating they did not allow dogs on the course, even if it was a service dog. I explained the ADA law, but he stood firm in his decision. I knew I couldn't run the marathon alone due to my cognitive disabilities and the risk of getting disoriented and going off course. I usually ran at the back of the pack, where there were not many people around to guide me.

I spoke with a friend who was knowledgeable about services for the disabled, including advocacy services, and contacted a local agency whose main purpose was to advocate for people who have disabilities to be sure they are included in situations and not prevented from doing things that healthy people could do on their own. They agreed to investigate the situation. After a lot of going back and forth, they did contact someone in Washington, DC, a person who had been part of the committee that created the ADA. She agreed that they were breaking the law and that I was protected under the law.

The race committee claimed their insurance company set the parameters regarding what they would cover and their liability if there was an issue with a dog on the course. As the handler, I assured them I would take full responsibility for my service dog. Despite communicating this, they stood their ground. When a runner registers for any race, they must sign a consent form releasing the race from liability for any injury or incident that occurs on the course. I reminded them that I had signed this release, yet they still refused. Shortly after this incident, the race was canceled due to Covid-19. I had to think quickly and draw deeply from my skills toolkit. I didn't know how long I would remain in this positive physical, psychological, and cognitive state. Experienced individuals with psychiatric illnesses learn to make the most of their periods of wellness, or "remission." Uncertain of how long this positive window would last, I knew it was essential to seize the moment, prepare, and be as productive as possible. Vince Lombardi, the legendary American football coach, says, "It's not whether you get knocked down, it's whether you get up." What else could I do but run?

I reached out to a few experienced marathon runners for advice. During Covid-19, all races were canceled, but virtual races became a popular alternative. You would register, run the race distance, and then submit your time to the committee. If the race committee wouldn't allow me to participate, I decided to run it virtually. The only challenge was that I had never trained for a marathon before, and I wasn't sure if Teddy was up for it. He was only five years old, but I figured that if I gradually increased our weekly distance, his system would adjust just as mine would. I shared my goal with my friend and coach, Joe, and the other runners in my group.

They were all incredibly supportive. I remembered how my dad ran the Marine Corps Marathon and how inspired I felt to follow in his footsteps. My sister also became a marathoner, running the New York, Chicago, and Marine Corps Marathons. I wanted to be like them. I wanted to feel accomplished and good about who I am. I've always struggled with low self-esteem, constantly putting myself down and focusing on my flaws.

Therapists could do countless exercises with me to improve my self-esteem, but they were never successful. This deep-seated belief that everyone around me is better, smarter, more outgoing, and special than I am, is something I've never been able to shake. Despite this, I keep taking on projects that I hope will help me feel fulfilled and prove to myself that maybe I'm not so worthless after all. The training was grueling and challenging. The race was in October, so it would be during the summer that I would have to increase my long runs up to 18 and 20 miles. The heat was certainly an issue, not just for me but also for Teddy, who I did not want to put in danger of heatstroke. We ran most of our miles along a paved trail that ran parallel to the river. With every training run, I would let him go into the river several times to cool off and have a healthy drink so he would not get dehydrated. I was also concerned about dehydration, especially because the temperature on the course would increase drastically once we reached the city streets included in the course.

I had never been an early riser. I usually slept late due to night terrors that left me drained. So, waking up at the crack of dawn was a significant challenge. However, it became the only strategy to minimize our exposure to the sun and heat. As the distance increased each week, we began to rise earlier and earlier. Sometimes we would get up as early as 3:00 or 4:00 am. Preparing for each run involved gathering my equipment, hydration pack, and essentials for Teddy. This process was particularly time-consuming due to my memory issues from ECT treatments. I had to make sure I didn't forget anything, such as sunscreen, my own water, fuel packets, and other necessary items to be fully prepared for long runs.

The shorter runs made me feel amazing. Once I exceeded five miles or so, I would just fall into a comfortable pace where I felt like I could run forever. This was the best part about running. Every runner knows what that feels like. During the first few miles, you are just trying to stabilize your breathing and pace. For me, at about mile four, I reach a sweet spot where I feel like I am effortlessly gliding along the course, with the feeling that I could continue for eternity. I love that sweet spot. I would finally feel calm and relaxed, and all the stress I was feeling would simply disappear from my body and mind. I maintained a steady pace, avoiding pushing myself too hard, knowing that I still had a marathon to finish. It was essential to gradually build my stamina each week. Running a marathon requires careful planning, and preparation should be taken very seriously. Starting off slowly was crucial to ensuring I wouldn't run out of energy later in the race.

We ran three or four times during the week and then our long runs on Saturdays or Sundays. Running wasn't just the issue, but resting my body and Teddy's body was also necessary to prevent any injuries. I needed Teddy to run with me, so I was especially careful and mindful of his health as well. I watched his every move. I was confident in Teddy's capability to run so far and long. He was part Border Collie; thus, I knew that he was a herding dog and bred for endurance. Herding dogs are capable of running all day in pastures, managing cattle, sheep, or goats, depending on the farmer's needs. That at least gave me some peace that I wasn't pushing him beyond his capabilities.

I would get comments from people saying, "You are going to make your dog run how far?" Everyone was so concerned about the dog. He had herding in his ancestry, so he definitely had the DNA and stamina to run 26 miles. I told people that they should be more concerned about me than about my dog. For my four-legged companion, this was a cake walk. He just trotted along next to me the entire time, as if he could easily do it all day. We would return home on many long-run days, and then he would still have the energy to be playful and bounce around. I wanted to lie down for at least two days, and he still wanted to play. It was definitely me that people needed to worry about.

Finding a balance between resting my body and giving my brain the rest it desperately needed during training for the marathon was a real struggle. It might sound odd to anyone unfamiliar with the complexities of living with a brain injury. But brain injuries, at least in my experience, drain energy just by staying alert and going through the motions of a typical day. Imagine this: I wake up, trying to orient myself. I have to figure out where I am physically, reassure myself that the nightmare wasn't real, piece together what I did yesterday, check if there's anything on the calendar for today, and then decide what clothes I have that are clean and go well together.

All of this happens before I've even started my day. Getting out of bed demands an enormous amount of energy, especially after I've already exhausted myself just by getting oriented to the day. During the spring or fall, it's a little easier, but in the colder months, my body bombards my brain with messages that it's too cold to move, urging me to stay under the covers. More often than not, I give in, especially when I'm lacking motivation. But on the days I manage to push through, my first priority is breakfast and taking my medication right away.

On top of everything else, living with narcolepsy leaves me vulnerable to intense daytime sleepiness. Because I don't get quality sleep at night, I constantly feel drowsy throughout the day and need to take frequent naps. It is as if, out of nowhere, while I'm in the middle of a project or cleaning, an overwhelming urge to close my eyes and sleep takes over. This is why I can't afford to forget my morning pills, because one of them actually keeps me awake. On days when I forget to take my

medication, I end up bedridden for two days, trying to let my body and mind recover. Managing depression, or any mental illness like anxiety, schizophrenia, bipolar disorder, or psychosis, is a daily struggle and overwhelming chore.

Whether I leave the house on any given day depends entirely on how my brain feels and what my mood is like. If my anxiety isn't overwhelming, I might venture out for quick errands or attend church. On better days, I take Teddy for a walk on one of the many trails near my house, using the opportunity to reinforce his training. He often tries to get away with not sitting and staying! These days are usually brighter because we both get out of the house, soaking up some sunlight and getting the exercise we need. But the energy I spend just getting out of bed and doing these activities often backfires. As soon as I get home, I feel an overwhelming need to collapse into bed.

This is my reality now. I have to ration my limited energy and try to live a life. A life that's full of forgetfulness, depression, difficulty interpreting what people say (especially cashiers!), and constant anxiety about all of it. Amid everything else at that stage, I also committed to running a marathon with my dog. This decision wasn't just about physical preparation; it was also a mental battle every step of the way. Each day, I had to choose the marathon over my mental illness. Whoever said running is all in your head was absolutely right, especially in my case. My brain constantly told me to stop running for just a minute, then start again, while the healthier part of my mind encouraged me by saying that I've made it this far and should be proud. It felt like I had a devil on one shoulder and an angel on the other, locked in a daily argument.

Training for a marathon is a complex, all-encompassing endeavor that demands meticulous planning and discipline. Staying hydrated requires careful attention to your water intake, while your diet needs to be adjusted to include more protein and complex carbohydrates. It's crucial to stay ahead of your training schedule, always knowing what's next so you can prepare accordingly. For instance, I aimed to complete my longer runs on Saturdays, but when that wasn't possible, Sundays became my backup. These extended runs were particularly challenging during the summer, as running 18 miles in 80-90 degree heat with my black-coated dog was far from ideal.

Training for long runs consumed nearly the entire day. Mornings began at 4:30 a.m., starting with a solid breakfast, despite the challenges my eating disorder posed. Afterward, I'd endure frequent trips to the

bathroom because of all the water I had consumed the day before. Dressing appropriately for the weather was a delicate balance, requiring clothes that were neither too cold nor too hot. Preparing my running bag remained a constant challenge, especially with my short-term memory issues, which seemed to surface at the worst times. I often misplaced essential items, such as Teddy's water bottle, only realizing too late that I had used it elsewhere and forgotten to put it back. Once everything was finally in place, Teddy and I would head out for hours of running. Afterward, I spent at least half an hour at the car, rehydrating with Gatorade while letting Teddy cool off in the river. By the time I got home, exhaustion would set in, leaving me torn between taking a shower or collapsing straight into bed.

Planning to run a marathon felt like an uphill battle. My motivation was low, which only worsened as my poor memory added to the frustration. The early morning hour offered no encouragement, and the lack of anyone to cheer me on made it even harder. To top it off, I was still searching for items I had somehow misplaced. As I continued to run longer distances, I found myself accumulating more gear to improve my performance. We've all experienced this. I bought new running gloves, hats, shirts, and tights. My running bag grew substantially to fit all these items, preparing for any situation where I might need a replacement for something I've forgotten.

However, with more gear came the challenge of sorting through everything to find what I need, which led to a daily search for misplaced items. I was accustomed to losing my wallet and glasses. My speech therapist helped me by suggesting that I keep these items in the same place every time, making them easier to find. This experience parallels the challenges employees face in meeting job demands, such as arriving on time to avoid being fired. Planning and training for a marathon felt like a demanding job that required mastering multitasking, a skill I initially struggled with. Despite these challenges, I persevered with determination.

Just a side note on my writing and how my brain functions; if you haven't noticed, I really digressed from talking about Teddy and preparing for my long runs. That's just how my brain works. When a thought pops up, I have to share it right away, or I'll forget it completely. My mind can only focus on one thing at a time, making it hard to switch back and forth during conversations or interactions. That's why Teddy is so important to me. I talk to him all day long, and as long as I show him love, he'll always be by my side. Teddy has become synonymous with running and with the things that help me live my life as fully as possible. He gets excited for every run; the moment he hears the word "run," he races up and down the hall, leaping around in joyful circles. This enthusiasm is the encouragement I need to tackle those long runs. I rely on his eagerness to run because I would do anything for him. He is like my child, and his loyalty to me is unwavering, and I reciprocate that loyalty. It's impossible not to get excited about running when this large, black bundle of energy starts spinning in circles, fully aware of the adventure that awaits.

I had lots of funny moments as well during training. One time, after a long run, I had to drive to see my parents. As soon as I arrived home, I was back out the door for a two-hour drive. That day, I learned a valuable lesson: never embark on a long trip right after a long run, unless you want to risk a near disaster. I was so desperate to pee that I could hardly hold it in. I tried everything, from tightening my muscles to doing Kegel exercises, but nothing seemed to help.

As I neared my parents' house, I called my dad and told him to clear the way because I needed to get to the bathroom immediately. The relief I felt when I finally sat on that toilet was indescribable. I must have peed for two solid minutes. When I came out of the bathroom, my dad gave me a knowing look. Being a seasoned runner himself, he understood all too well the constant need to find a bathroom. Ask any runner, and they will have plenty of stories about the urgency to relieve themselves. We are so accustomed to it that ducking into the nearest patch of woods becomes nothing to be ashamed of.

Planning and training for the marathon was something I could never have done on my own. I'm incredibly grateful for my running family, who took on the essential tasks of coordinating our routes, ensuring our safety, and always being there if I needed anything. My friends Deb and Dawn were particularly amazing. They often rose at dawn to ride their bicycles beside me, guiding me through turns and managing traffic so we could focus on the run without worrying about cars. Their energy was infectious; it was impossible not to feel motivated with them by my side. They carried backpacks filled with fuel and water, ready to provide whatever I needed, whenever I needed it. Running is a very social activity, especially the marathon preparation training runs. Everyone knows I'm the one who never stops talking while running, and it helped having people to talk to during the long runs. We shared stories, cracked jokes, and sang along to the playlist Deb had specially curated for my marathon.

They even brought extra water so I could thoroughly cool down Teddy. We made frequent stops along the river,

allowing him to wade into the water, fully immerse himself, and drink to his heart's content. It was these friends, along with my wonderful family, who kept me encouraged every step of the way. Sure, getting out of bed was always a struggle, but with a loving and supportive network, it became easier. As race day approached, my excitement grew, though so did my hesitation. I had a deadline to meet, and my obsessive-compulsive personality disorder was determined to ensure I followed my training regimen to the letter.

There were moments when I broke down in tears, overwhelmed by self-doubt, wondering how I ever believed I could do this. This wasn't just a short run down the block; this was 26.2 miles. Hours of running lay ahead of me, and, at my slow pace, it felt even more daunting. On top of that, I had to constantly prioritize Teddy's needs, ensuring he didn't get injured or overheated. The weight of it all sometimes felt unbearable. Was I kidding myself? I knew people who had run marathons, and I had always admired them, but this felt different.

My brain was severely compromised. I struggled to solve even the smallest problems, and when I did attempt a solution, I rarely considered all the potential dangers. The constant "brain noise" drained me and made everything feel overwhelming. Thankfully, I had friends who joined me on my training runs, so I did not have to face it alone. Their company helped drown out the noise in my head and gave me a much-needed mental break. They guided me, telling me when to turn left or right. Without them, I would have ended up in New Jersey!

Sometimes on the runs certain things did look familiar, like the charming house that resembles a dollhouse. It is painted light blue with white shutters, a beautiful white porch, rocking chairs, and houseplants adding a touch of warmth. Or the tiny wishing well that stands in the middle of another house's front yard, white and gray with flowers blooming from inside the well. I could remember these details for a fleeting moment before the memory slipped away. Whether that thought ever returned is in the hands of the Almighty. My mind feels like a puzzle, with pieces scattered, and every day I try to fit them together. Usually, it is not a life-altering situation, but when I am put on the spot, my anxiety surges, clouding my thoughts just when I need clarity the most to complete the task. I needed clarity to attain my goal of running a marathon, but I had the support I needed to reach my destination.

Crossing the Finish Line: Victory and Embracing the Joy of the Journey

O n the day of the marathon, I was up before sunrise. For long runs, I always wake up two hours early to give myself ample time to prepare. Rushing on race day only increases the chances of forgetting something crucial. To avoid this, I had meticulously written out a lengthy checklist that covered everything except the kitchen sink: bandages, KT tape, ankle braces, hats, headbands, plenty of water, and, of course, Gatorade. I made sure to pack my salt pills to prevent dehydration and stocked up on "Runner" jelly beans from Jelly Belly. I had been using these sports beans for about a year, so I knew they wouldn't upset my stomach.

As I prepared my water pack, I glanced over and saw Teddy sitting upright, his face lit up with a huge grin. I had purposely delayed putting on my sneakers, knowing it would instantly tip him off that a run was in the works. But Teddy was onto me. The moment I grabbed my socks and sneakers, he sprang to his feet, his tail wagging furiously as if to say, "Hurry up already; I'm ready to run!" In the car, he couldn't stop whining and whimpering, fully aware that today was the big day.

Paul and I had the car packed, and I insisted on driving. Normally, I'd let him take the wheel, but today was different. Today was my day, and I needed to be in complete control. After a brief "discussion," he reluctantly settled into the passenger seat, grumbling under his breath. With our seatbelts fastened, I took a long, deep breath, exhaled slowly, and said, "Let's go." We were off to the start of the marathon, about 45 minutes away. The race was set on a RailTrail, one of those old railroad tracks converted into hiking trails. I had run on many of them before, each offering its own unique beauty and serenity.

A close friend, Amy, and her husband met us at the starting line on the top of the vast, boundless mountain. Amy would run the first seven miles down the trail with me. We had shared many hiking and camping trips with her and the children. I always loved it because of the connection to nature. I thought it was only fitting that Amy and I would run the trail together, side by side. Everywhere we looked, there were bright shades of orange, green, yellow, and red just looking back at us as if to say, "Come and experience God's majestic beauty."

Dawn was also a good friend from my running group who joined us on this journey. She was more of a cyclist than a runner. I was thrilled that she would ride with us. The most important thing was that she had a backpack full of water, fuel, bananas, M&M's, and whatever else she could think of that we might need. I think the plan was for her to go with us up to about mile 17. Thanks to the ECT, I can't remember some of the specifics from that day. She had a monster of a bike with all the bells and whistles.

Our close friends, Deb and her husband, Greg, played a significant role in planning the marathon. They meticulously measured the course multiple times to ensure it totaled 26.2 miles. We had to avoid certain roads due to traffic, prioritizing our safety. Although Deb couldn't be there on marathon day, she was very much with us in spirit. Having run with her many times before, I knew how disappointed she was to miss the big day. Before we set out on our adventure, I kissed my family

goodbye and handed them a note I had scribbled in my journal. The note included all the stops where they could meet us and an estimated time of arrival.

Since I had never run this many miles at once, I decided to play it safe with a steady 13:00 minute/mile pace, neither too fast nor too slow. We certainly didn't start with a sprint; it was a comfortable, easy pace. Early in the race, my pace was right on target, but as the miles passed, I found myself slowing down. Dawn, Amy, and I enjoyed our jog down the mountain, being captivated by the breathtaking scenery that resembled a Bob Ross painting. I could hear his soothing voice in my mind, "And maybe there will be just a little tree popping up here beside the gentle flow of the river right HERE."

In high school, while waiting for the bus, I would watch Bob Ross on TV with my dad, who was also waiting to go to work. We must have watched him paint hundreds of pictures together. He always had such a calm and peaceful voice that matched the feeling you would get when seeing him create his own "work of art." Paul and Amy's husband, Tim, met us at the bottom of the trail right on the other side of a small park with colorful swings, a climbing gym, and plenty of benches for the moms and dads to keep an eye on their children.

As we arrived at the park, I mentally ticked off another milestone: "Seven miles down, only 19 more to go!" Waiting at the base of the trail was my friend MaryAnn, who had been a cornerstone during my training runs. She was prepared to accompany me for the next 12 miles, the longest stretch anyone would run with me that day. MaryAnn was by her car, adjusting her running vest, when I suddenly realized that I had forgotten something crucial: fuel! I had forgotten one thing that was essential for me to have if I was going to run and finish the entire 26.2 miles. For long-distance running, it's essential to keep your body energized with items like gels or "goos." It's like liquid energy in a gel form in different flavors like jellybeans, M&M, or even Swedish Fish. But in my pre-race nerves, I had completely overlooked packing my own.

Thankfully, MaryAnn had everything I needed and more right there in her car. She was so well prepared, it was as if she had packed for a trip to Disney and back with her grandchildren! As soon as we left the parking lot with Teddy, we rounded a bend to get away from the gas station. Just as we stepped off the trail behind the building, we found ourselves face-to-face with a tall, disheveled man who looked worse for wear. He was yelling at us, slurring his words, and flailing around, but we had no idea why.

Suddenly, he jumped out of his beat-up car, and for a moment, it seemed like he might come after us. But knowing my husband and our friends were just around the corner, and with Teddy, our big black dog with a fierce "don't mess with me" bark, I felt confident we were safe. As the man kept yelling, I couldn't resist egging him on a little, feeling secure with Teddy by our side. Teddy, standing tall with his hair bristling and ears perked, let out one powerful bark. That was all it took for the man to turn around and scramble back into his car. We honestly thought he might come after us, but as we got further away, we stopped for a bit and couldn't help but laugh about the whole situation. I laughed so hard my belly started to ache!

The next ten miles were peaceful as we jogged through the small towns nestled in what locals call "The Valley." It was still incredibly early in the morning, so the only people who were awake were the ones being good Christians and on their way to church. I prayed for a full seven days before this run, and I think that I was good with God! Dawn had a small speaker attached to her bike, and we moved to the rhythm of the music. She played a great mix of tunes from the 1980s and even some from earlier decades. I love running to music, but there's one catch: I tend to match my pace to the beat. This wasn't an issue until a really fast song came on, and I found myself struggling to keep up. One minute I was jogging slowly to *Amazing Grace*, and the next I was sprinting to Elvis' *Jailhouse Rock*!

We had so much fun, filled with singing, dancing, and sharing stories as we went along. We, but especially me, loved admiring the different homes, imagining which ones I wouldn't mind living in. The houses that caught my eye were the ones with charming white front porches, adorned with plants, and, of course, classic white rocking chairs. I wanted all of those things, though I didn't have them at my own home. But it's always nice to dream! By that time, we were regularly drinking from our water packs and eating the fuel that MaryAnn brought. Paul, Amy, Tim, and James met us at different points on the course. We had to water Teddy down so he wouldn't overheat. This was important because we were no longer next to the river, where I would usually command him to go in the water to cool off. Whenever we stopped at someone's car, we would refuel and water Teddy down. It was amazing how many people had chipped in to make this marathon come to fruition.

At one point we were almost passing by a bowling alley parking lot. I had already arranged with Paul to meet us there. When we arrived, there was a small table with

food and water. Teddy excitedly jumped in the car to rest! There was just one problem... that was not our car! Apparently, another avid runner had decided to do his own virtual marathon on the same day. His wife was also setting up water stops for him. I dragged Teddy out of her car as we were all bending over laughing uncontrollably. We looked over, and 50 feet away was the car we were supposed to have gone to. Needless to say, there was a lot of laughter.

We wanted to run, but we also wanted to have fun doing it! As we passed through small towns, we came upon another trailhead, where a group of our running friends awaited us. Among them was someone I affectionately call Mama Ginny. She's in her 70s (I think) and still tackles half marathons with unwavering energy. Mama Ginny is a constant source of inspiration to me, always full of life as she runs, bikes, and cares for her grandchildren. She's been a steady presence, always ready with a supportive hug when I've needed it. I can only hope I'll still be running with her spirit when I reach her age.

The Pandemic Express, my running group during Covid-19, was also waiting for my arrival. With official running programs on hold due to the chaos surrounding Covid-19, we decided to keep running together outdoors, believing that the fresh air would keep us safe from spreading or catching the virus. While others stayed indoors with their masks on, we were outside, enjoying the open air and snapping pictures to document our runs. The Pandemic Express was a fun and spirited group, and our coach Joe always made sure the routes were varied and enjoyable. During the holidays, we would often spot beautifully decorated houses, and without hesitation, we would all pose on their lawns for a picture with the festive lights. It was not just about running; it was about having fun while doing it. That was the positive and optimistic Pandemic Express mindset that we all needed to get through the pandemic.

This was an incredible group of friends. Joe was in front, jumping up and down, calling out to me and Teddy by name. They had signs that said, "Go Teddy and Lisa!" and they were all geared up to run a few miles with us. We laughed and told stories, and they all just kept our spirits up to keep up that emotional energy and distract me from how tired I was really feeling! When I saw them waiting, I was overwhelmed by how many had come out just for me. I had always seen this as my personal goal, and I tend to be a private person, except for writing this book. But seeing them all so invested made me realize how much their support meant, and it felt wonderful to have more friends to share in the camaraderie.

Now we were right next to the river, almost at its edge. A paved path ran alongside it, but just off the trail, a steep downslope led directly to the water. I knew the usual spots where we stopped to let Teddy cool off, so a few times I took him off the leash and gave him the command to get in. He eagerly leaped into the river, drank his fill, then bounded back out to shake off in front of the whole group. I was used to this routine, but I think it caught the Pandemic Express by surprise! It was a long run, so people dropped out and others joined us as we made our way to one of the bigger parks. I knew I would see Paul and James there. I was excited to arrive and embrace them.

We, meaning Teddy, MaryAnn, Joe, Jay, Kathy, Rob, and a few more, were approaching the park, and I could clearly see Paul and James. Standing next to them were my sister and my dad. I never understood what they meant when people would say they "jumped for joy," but I certainly understood then. They visibly jumped for joy! I had wondered if my dad would make the trip from home, and of course my dad never disappoints, especially when it comes to seeing "one of *his* girls" running. I hugged them and cried. I had to keep going. I was on a roll, so I didn't want to lose momentum. A group of people paused their run at that point, but then Joe joined in again!

We set off again, taking the wooded path to yet another park where my marathon coach, Pat, awaited us. There's something about Pat that's impossible not to like. He's the very image of a leprechaun, with his bright red hair, boundless energy, and a knack for storytelling. I loved listening to his countless tales of running and other adventures. Now, with Joe and Pat by my side, we left the cool, shaded trail and returned to the scorching pavement. The sun beat down on my face, and I could feel my pace slow down, but I wasn't chasing a personal record on this run. My goal was simple: to complete the full 26.2 miles, and that's exactly what I intended to do.

"If you can't fly, then run. If you can't run, then walk.
If you can't walk, then crawl. But by all means, keep moving."
~Martin Luther King, Jr.

On the bustling city streets, Joe and Pat skillfully managed traffic, allowing me to cross without breaking my stride. But after just a couple of miles, my left ankle gave out, sending a sharp pain shooting up my leg from ankle to thigh. Pat, ever the calm presence, simply said, "Alright, let's walk it off, nice and easy." So, that's what we did, but I knew I couldn't push through another four miles with this kind of pain. Then, like a flash, I had a rare but timely epiphany. Just a few weeks earlier, I had lent my ankle brace to my friend Amy. As I continued running, I pulled out my cell phone and called Amy to see if she still had that brace. To my relief, not only did she have it, but she was wearing it! I asked her to take it off so I could put it on at our next stop, where everyone would be waiting.

The pain in my foot was so sharp that I had to walk most of that part of the course. When we arrived at the industrial park, the cars were already there, and Amy had the back hatch of her car open. I quickly took off my shoe and sock, put on the brace, and then slipped my sock and shoe back on. The relief was almost instant. I was so happy – I could run again, and it felt so much better.

Now it was just Joe, Pat, and Terry with me for the final few miles. Terry ran right beside me, keeping my mind occupied with stories from our childhood and the funny things we did without our parents' knowledge. It was a perfect way to catch up, with no distractions from a larger crowd. Meanwhile, Joe and Pat, our own little peanut gallery, were hysterical, but I knew I needed to stay focused on the road ahead. Joe, ever the spontaneous one, was true to form, always living in the moment and a fly by the seat of his pants kind of guy. Since it was October, many people already had their Halloween decorations up in their yards, and Joe was nagging (he does that a lot) me to take a picture in front of a house that had a huge 15-foot skeleton in the yard. I thought to myself that I'm only running this marathon once, so why not? Joe, who was part human and part photographer, obviously took the opportunity to take a couple of pictures.

With about two miles left, the sky opened, and the rain came pouring down. We huddled under a bridge for a few minutes, but when it became clear the rain wasn't letting up, I decided to push on and finish the race. Unbeknownst to me at the time, Joe leaned over and whispered to Pat, "Can't you speed this up? I've got a news crew waiting for us at the courthouse." Pat told me about this later. If I'd heard Joe say that while I was still running, I might have just punched him! Joe had been dropping hints all along about a surprise waiting for me at the courthouse, where the run would end. He's like a little boy who can't keep a secret, practically bursting with excitement. At first, his nonstop chatter was fine, especially around mile 20, but by mile 24, he was really starting to get on my nerves. I finally yelled at the "peanut gallery" to please just "shut up" so I could focus on finishing. Pat, ever the great coach and voice of reason, usually kept things in check, but once Joe starts talking, all you'll hear is laughter.

To my amazement, Teddy was still in peak condition. His run had settled into a steady trot, and he kept pace effortlessly, as if this were just another routine training session. At five years old, he was in his prime, the most loyal and intuitive dog I'd ever known. Teddy and I shared a deep connection, almost as if he could read my thoughts. He had an uncanny ability to sense my stress and emotions, always responding with exactly what I needed. He looked so content, enjoying the simple pleasure of a jog outdoors.

We were now approaching a hill that every runner in the area knew all too well. I had tackled it many times during training, but never with 24 miles already behind me. The hill was steep and winding, and up to this point, I had managed to run up every incline on the course. Taking a deep breath, we began to jog steadily uphill. Our running friends knew this hill well, and many had gathered around, waving signs, ringing cowbells, and holding balloons, all there to cheer on Teddy and me. I was huffing and puffing, doing everything I could not to collapse in front of everyone.

What I really wanted at that stage was to be able to breathe! I was amazed at how many wonderful people there were in my life. Never could I have imagined that this many people would show up just for me. I just couldn't fathom so many people were here because they loved me and supported me. They all knew of my psychiatric sagas and were aware of the brain injury I sustained following the shock treatments. Coming from a shy and introverted little girl to this was quite the transformation.

I felt so full of love that the hill was nothing compared to how great I felt. We were now in the final mile, and I could barely see as the rain poured down in sheets. Then, as if by some miracle, the sun broke through the clouds! At the top of the hill, one of my friends, let's call her JessePA, was waiting in her car, ready to drive ahead and escort me to the courthouse. It felt surreal, like I was one of those elite runners in the New York Marathon, complete with my own escort and people snapping photos from every direction!

My sister Terry stayed by my side, talking to me and coaching me all the way to the end. We faced one last challenge, a massive hill that was one of the area's most famous. I took a deep breath and pushed forward, step by step. More friends were waiting on that hill, knowing the finish line was just beyond it. I couldn't give up now, not after all the hard training, with the clock ticking down. This hill was tricky because the beginning was steep, but then it stretched into a gradual and relentless climb until the other side finally came into view. Friends and fellow

runners surrounded me, cheering, "You can do it, Lisa! Keep going!" But it was Teddy who stole the show, with the crowd's cheers for him far outnumbering those for me. He always captured everyone's attention long before they noticed me! We made it to the top of the hill, and to my amazement, there were 40-50 people clapping and cheering for Lisa and Teddy.

By this point, a few friends had joined me, ready to run with me to the finish line. It was a tradition in our running group that when someone was struggling, the stronger runners would go back, meet them, and run with them to the finish. The whole experience felt like a dream. I couldn't believe what I was witnessing! Not only that I had almost completed 26.2 miles, but that so many people cared enough to show up and cheer me on.

Now it was the last 50 yards, and it was all downhill. I could see the courthouse and lots of people and balloons. And thanks to my awesome coach, a news crew as well. He always had something up his sleeve! I got to the courthouse and immediately ran into the arms of my 19-year-old son, James. We were extremely close emotionally. He had endured the same hardships as me over the years while I underwent those treatments. He always told me that I had to do what I had to do to stay healthy. He was and is still most definitely wise beyond his years! All he said to me was, "I'm proud of you, Mama." That's all I needed to hear. I hugged and kissed Paul and my dad, who whispered in my ear, "THAT'S MY GIRL." That will reverberate in my mind for the rest of my life. That was always his term when he was exceedingly proud of Terry and me. That's exactly the voice I wanted to hear at the end of 26.2 miles.

Dad was a runner for years. He was the one who got me started on this when I was only 15. This was him passing on the baton, and I was proud to carry it. I made the traditional post-race phone call to my mom, who I knew was at home, worried and anxiously waiting for the phone to ring. The moment I heard her voice, I burst into tears. She had been traumatized and through so much when I was sick, and on top of the depression, she had to cope with the unexpected brain injury. She knew that as long as I was running regularly, my cognitive symptoms stayed manageable. Maybe all that blood flow to my brain was helping it function better. I can't explain it, but I accept it for all it's worth. Every time we talked, she would ask if I had run that day. If I said no, I reassured her that I would most definitely run the next day. She needed that reassurance, and it was good because she kept me accountable.

Paul enveloped me in the biggest bear hug, followed by a compassionate kiss that resonated deep

in my heart as he whispered, "I knew you could do it all along." As I embraced everyone around me, we were reminded that the news crew had been waiting to capture this special moment for a while. They filmed us crossing the finish line and then asked if they could interview us. My family and I stood together as the newsman began asking questions. Meanwhile, Teddy, completely uninterested in the commotion, rolled around on his back, his energy boundless, as if he were playing in a pile of leaves. He was still having the time of his life! I can't recall all the questions the newsman asked, but I remember that he wanted to know whether I had a message for anyone watching. The only thing I could say was that if I could achieve this goal after years of battling depression and facing many other challenges, then anyone could. It all begins with taking that first step.

"There is a past version of you that is proud
of how far you have come." ~Anonymous

I was stunned to see my dear and very special friend Susan at the finish line, I couldn't believe my eyes. It had been a long time since we'd seen each other, as she was bravely battling colorectal cancer, and I knew her fight was growing more difficult. Despite her small stature, her radiant smile was all I needed to see. She hugged me tightly and told me she always knew I could do it. With her characteristic wisdom, she reminded me that life is a battle, and we all have our own struggles to face. She said that by winning this battle, I had gained the strength to face many more in the future. She blessed me with a medal she had received at a cancer retreat. It was adorned with a single but powerful word: HOPE.

Voices for Change: Treating the Wounds and Fighting Lifelong Scars

"One of the lessons that I grew up with was to always stay true to yourself and never let what someone else says distract you from your goals." ~Michelle Obama

I am thrilled and truly grateful that you would consider reading about my story and my struggles, and that you even made it to this chapter. But you didn't read this book for me. You read it for yourself, to better understand the trauma of someone you care about, or perhaps as a professional seeking to deepen your understanding of what your patients or clients experience during depressive episodes or when they turn to you for help. This book does not suggest that getting a dog or running a marathon will magically make all your troubles disappear. Life doesn't work that way, and neither does mental illness.

I continue to struggle with bipolar depression, anxiety, and the cognitive side effects that came with the ECT treatments. However, both my family and I noticed a significant improvement in my symptoms once I began running consistently. Running a few miles one week and then a few more the next didn't make much difference. The key was consistency, allowing my body and brain to reap the full benefits of the activity. For me, running made a real impact. I believe the increased blood flow throughout my body, especially to my brain, helped alleviate some of the challenges I faced with thinking, planning, and processing. Although those difficulties remained, they became more manageable.

There have been several times when I injured my ankle or pulled a muscle, forcing me to rest for a few weeks to prevent the injury from worsening. During these periods, I noticed something unsettling: my cognitive problems seemed to temporarily worsen when I stopped running. It's strange to experience mental clarity one day (though running doesn't entirely solve the problem; it makes it manageable) and then, after a few days or a week, find myself back where I was when I first started ECT treatments. My memory becomes ten times worse,

I struggle to spell or find the right words, my headaches intensify, and I spend more time in bed. I misplace things even more than before, can only handle one-step activities, become overwhelmed by the smallest tasks, and start isolating from my family again.

Running didn't completely solve my problem, but it did lead to healthier eating habits, which definitely had a positive impact on my overall cognitive well-being. For you, it might be walking, swimming, cycling, or whatever activity interests you. I find it incredibly therapeutic just to get out of the house, and Teddy helped me do that. Often, it's as simple as getting outside to feel the fresh air. I also experience seasonal affective disorder, like many others. This means that during the winter months, with less sunlight, I'm more prone to feeling depressed and sad. My worst months are from November to March, but once March arrives, I can bundle up and go for a short walk, unless it's 10 degrees out.

One year, I got a treadmill so I could keep running during the winter months, and it has been an absolute godsend. It is much cheaper than paying $80,000 to the hospital, $40,000 to the anesthesiologist, and even more to the psychiatrist. My husband gives me perspective and helps me see things more clearly. Interestingly, I have recently come across studies that confirm exercise can have the same effect as an antidepressant. I wish I had known that 30 years ago. The purpose of writing this book isn't driven by the need for fame or fortune. Don't get me wrong, the money would certainly help since living off Social Security is laughable at best. But that's not what this is about. The real reason I'm putting these words on paper is to remind you that you're not alone, no matter how isolated you might feel.

As David Mitchell says, "You are allowed to feel messed up inside and out. It doesn't mean you're defective – it just means you are human." Depression is a master of deception, convincing you that you're stranded in a world that's ignorant and indifferent to your pain. But the truth is, over 280 million people worldwide are battling the same demons, according to the World Health Organization. You feel alone because that's depression's cruel trick. It wants to cut you off from everyone you know and love, making you believe that no one could possibly understand the weight of your struggles. I'm here to tell you: you are not alone.

Paul and I have always been upfront and honest with our loved ones about where I was at psychologically. We never hid it from family, friends, or even our son as he grew up. I like to think that the love and support we received was a result of this, because we let people in on what was really happening. But that didn't mean things were always smooth between us. We had plenty of arguments over trivial things, which were related to how hard it was for him to see me struggling day after day.

It's important for our loved ones to have their own outlets for the feelings of helplessness they experience. It might be the need for a friend, a therapist, or a support group, whether in person or online. If they hold in their own feelings of hopelessness, the situation only becomes more intense for everyone involved. Your friends and family can't help you if you don't let them in on what's happening. They notice the changes, like the way you speak, how you skip meals, how you sleep through most of the day, and how you miss work. They see it all and feel helpless too.

Paul often complained that I didn't share what I was going through, but the truth is, I didn't fully understand it myself. I knew how I felt, but finding the words to express that was nearly impossible. There aren't words strong enough to convey the depth of hopelessness I feel when I'm at my worst. So there we were, the two of us together, not knowing what was going on. All we really needed to do was reach out. When I was in the hospital, friends and family stepped in to help by making meals for Paul and our son. Someone always had to watch James so Paul could visit me during visiting hours. If you don't speak up about your needs, no one will know what they are. Depression is an invisible illness. Just look at me; I can run marathons and half marathons, but I can't recall the three words you asked me to remember just five minutes ago. You have to be your own best advocate.

My hope is that this book reaches as many caregivers, therapists, and families as possible. At best, they struggle to understand the internal challenges of the people they care for and love who battle mental illnesses. How can they possibly understand the way your mind works? To them, it makes no sense, but maybe this book can help people begin to grasp the kinds of thoughts that race through our minds every day. To them, it is not logical. But that is the nature of mental illness. Nothing about it is logical, and that is precisely what makes it so challenging.

Another reason for writing this book is to raise awareness that ECT is still being administered in hospitals today. Shockingly, it is also performed on teenagers and often on elderly patients who may not have the cognitive ability to fully understand the gravity of the decision. Recently, I visited the website of the hospital where I received my treatments and searched for "ECT consent." The current consent form they use for ECT treatments didn't surprise me, but it deeply troubled me. It mentioned nothing about the long-term cognitive effects. It briefly touched on temporary short-term memory loss, headaches, and other minor issues that wouldn't seem to impede a person's ability to function normally.

Please encourage anyone you know who suffers from severe depression to read this book and consider the impact ECT has had on my life. Thousands of people around the world have also suffered from ECT, and they connect and support each other through Facebook groups. Many of them, like me, have reported numerous side effects to their psychiatrists, but they, too, have faced a lack of validation and inadequate support. I find comfort in knowing that I'm not alone in my suffering.

Many of them are burdened with anger and regret, feeling they were not fully informed or prepared for how ECT would profoundly change their lives, bringing negative consequences and lifelong challenges. Others share the same warnings and express deep regret about their decision to undergo the treatments. I present a few of their perspectives here, which resonate with my own experience:

Q "I will NEVER recommend it, and I will NEVER do it again! It has robbed me of things I will never get back, and that makes me so angry. I only did 11 treatments before I said no more because I was literally crying from fear as they took me in for another."

Q "If you're offered ECT, don't do it. You might be feeling terrible now, but it will pass. ECT wrecks lives, and you'll never get back what you've lost. Doctors lie about the side effects, and when you end up with a brain injury, no one will help you."

Q "I will always warn anybody about the effects of ECT, and I hope that in the future, people who have had ECT with terrible side effects will finally be recognized by the medical community."

Q "I regret my decision to do ECT. I stumble over my words and can't remember or retain any information. I have no emotions."

Q "Since my treatments, my world has been turned upside down. Nothing is the same."

Q "ECT changed the trajectory of my life. I lost 75% of three years of memory, and chunks of 3-12 years are lost. I've never regained that memory."

○ "ECT destroys lives... mine, yours... and everyone around you. It erases everything good. ECT leaves you in a fog that never clears."

○ "I have been so severely messed up by 38 ECT treatments that were given to me over a period of nine months. I told them I wanted to stop, but they discouraged it and tried to keep doing them."

Despite all the years I've spent voicing my concerns about my "ECT injury," no one listened, and this atrocity continues to be inflicted on people who have no idea how dangerous and life-altering these treatments can be. I want the world to know that ECT can indeed cause serious cognitive side effects, which may be permanent and can leave a person unable to fully function, comprehend, problem-solve, or make sound judgments. It can also rob them of years of cherished memories. I do not want what happened to me to happen to anyone else. I will tirelessly advocate for those who suffered from something inflicted upon them without proper warning, and I will continue to fervently discourage anyone from undergoing ECT. If I must be the voice and face that exposes the severe damage ECT can inflict on the brain, then brace yourself, because I will not back down.

Recently, I was referred to a neurologist due to some cognitive changes I've experienced. While the wait to see the neurologist directly is longer, I had the opportunity to meet with the Physician Assistant. She spent about an hour with us and recommended both physical therapy and speech therapy. I hadn't realized that speech therapists also focus significantly on cognitive rehabilitation for patients with concussions and even for children on the autism spectrum. Now, I have access to physical therapy to address my balance issues, speech therapy to help rewire my brain, and visual therapy to assist my brain in accurately processing visual information. I am deeply resentful that I wasn't given this help ten years ago. The resources were available, but no one, especially my psychiatrist, thought to refer me to a place where I could address the numerous cognitive side effects that have dominated and still control my life.

Change only happens when people unite to tell the world that something is failing and needs urgent attention. Through this book, I hope to inspire more people to find the courage to stand up and share their stories. Every person who has undergone ECT has a valuable story to tell. If you have suffered because of this, please consider sharing your story to shed light on this harmful procedure. As we reach the end of this journey together, my heartfelt wish for you is to find the strength and validation that have eluded you through the years of enduring the lasting side effects of ECT. Your story matters, and through sharing it, you will find the comfort and understanding that have long been sought. May you and your loved ones be blessed with the courage and resilience needed to navigate this challenging path and bring your souls to a place of peace.

"Promise me you will always remember: you are braver than you believe, stronger than you seem, and smarter than you think." —A.A. Milne, Winnie-the-Pooh

GOD, grant me the serenity to stop
beating myself up for not doing
things perfectly, the courage to
forgive myself because I'm working
on doing better, and the wisdom to
know that you already love me
just the way I am.

-Unknown

About Lisa A. Conway

Photo by Jake Danna Stevens for *The Times-Tribune*

Lisa A. Conway, MSW, is a strong Christian woman who carries her faith with her everywhere she goes. Throughout her young life she found herself being drawn towards helping those in need. She received her Bachelor of Arts Degrees in Psychology and Spanish from King's College in Wilkes-Barre, Pennsylvania.

Once she graduated and started working in the field of social services she decided she wanted to become a Licensed Social Worker. She received her Master of Social Work (MSW) from Marywood University in Scranton, Pennsylvania. She was awarded the Murray

Fox Practicum Educator's Award to merit her excellence in being a dedicated and effective field instructor.

Throughout her career she found herself working with the elderly and disabled, abused women and children, people battling addiction, the homeless, and had the privilege to work with the dying and their families at Hospice.

After suffering with mental illness for years, Lisa, herself needed intervention. Her psychiatrist encouraged her to get ECT treatments. She and her family suffered for years trying to manage the depression and the cognitive effects of the ECT.

Lisa and her service dog, Teddy, began running together and Lisa's depression began to lift, as well as some of the effects of the treatments.

After learning the truth about the damage the treatments did to her, she realized she was never warned about the cognitive damage the treatments could cause. Lisa needed to warn people about the damage it did to her.

It is Lisa's goal to offer compassion and support to those suffering from mental illness, education to their caregivers, both familial and professional and to bring the truth of the dangers of ECT to light and to advocate for all ECT survivors.

Resources / References
Places to Get Help

In Crisis Dial 988
Crisis Text Line 741741

BOOKS

Baugh, Robert. *My Life Rewired: Healing Childhood Traumas and Finding Purpose Post-Traumatic Brain Injury*. Inner Peace Press, 2024.

Bourne, Edmund J. *The Anxiety and Phobia Workbook*. New Harbinger Publications, 2020.

Goleman, Daniel. *Emotional Intelligence: Why It Can Matter More than IQ for Character, Health and Lifelong Achievement*. Bantam Books, 1995.

Khan, Anum, and Leon Edward. *CONCUSSION, TRAUMATIC BRAIN INJURY, mTBI ULTIMATE REHABILITATION GUIDE: Your Holistic Manual for Traumatic Brain Injury Rehabilitation and Care*. 2019.

Lohret, Amber. *Invisible: Finding Purpose and Spiritual Awakening After the Storm of Traumatic Brain Injury.* Inner Peace Press, 2024.

Mackenzie, Natalie. *Fatigue Management Journal: The Ultimate Tool for Managing Brain Injury Fatigue.* Independently published, 2021.

Newmark, Amy. *Chicken Soup for the Soul: Recovering from Traumatic Brain Injuries: 101 Stories of Hope, Healing, and Hard Work.* Chicken Soup for the Soul Publishing, 2014.

Scher, Amy B. *How to Heal Yourself from Depression When No One Else Can: A Self-Guided Program to Stop Feeling like Sh*t.* Sounds True, 2021.

Starr, Carole J. *To Root & to Rise: Accepting Brain Injury.* Spiral Path Publishing, 2017.

Trenton, Nick. *Stop Overthinking: 23 Techniques to Relieve Stress, Stop Negative Spirals, Declutter Your Mind, and Focus on the Present.* Pkcs Media, 2021.

Young, Sarah. *Jesus Calling: Enjoying Peace in His Presence.* Thomas Nelson, 2015.

WEBSITES

Brain Injury Association of America | https://www.biausa.org

National Institute of Mental Health | https://www.nimh/nih.gov

Help Guide (good for Care givers) | https://HelpGuide.org

National Alliance on Mental Illness | https://www.NAMI.org

Brain Injury Association of America | https://Biausa.org

10 Podcasts to listen to if you Struggle with Depression
https://www.Healthline.com

Psychology Today a Traumatic Brain Therapist
https://www.psychologytoday.com

FACEBOOK GROUPS

- Surviving Electroshock-International Support Group for ECT Survivors**
- Brain Injury Support Group-Life rewired
- Mental Health Awareness and Support
- The Brain Injury Therapist
- Brain Injury & Cognitive Rehabilitation Group
- Mental Health and Loneliness: self care, help and support for all
- Brain Injury Life & Struggles Support Group**

** Lisa found especially good support in these groups